Go Home and Tell

Go home to thy friends, and
tell them how great things
the Lord hath done for thee.
Mark 5:19

Go home and tell

BERTHA SMITH

BROADMAN PRESS
Nashville, Tennessee

Library of Congress Catalog Card Number: 65-10342
Printed in the United States of America

Introduction

Miss Bertha Smith was appointed in 1917 for missionary service in China by the Foreign Mission Board of the Southern Baptist Convention. She served in North China where, along with others, she experienced the great revival. This revival strengthened Baptist churches in Shantung Province and resulted in the conversion of many unbelievers and the transformation of many Christian workers.

Her book is a testimony of her experiences with her Lord in the responsibilities of missionary service and the dangers through which it was necessary to go, both during the time of war with Japan and the Communist upheaval in China.

In 1948 she was transferred to Taiwan as the first missionary of our Board on that island. Many other missionaries were assigned to that field, and the Taiwan Mission has grown to be one of the most fruitful and effective in the Orient.

This book reflects the vital faith of this missionary in her Lord and indicates the consequences of that faith in a life of service and victory. Those who read it will find it spiritually profitable.

BAKER JAMES CAUTHEN

Preface

This book has been written in response to suggestions by friends who have heard me relate incidents of answered prayer during my forty-one and a half years in China.

I have not depended upon my memory for anything related, even though all that I have written is still fresh in my mind. I have notes which were made at the time, and letters home in which the experiences were described.

I wish to thank my praying friends who upheld me as I sat at my typewriter a day here and there. I am deeply indebted to my college and seminary friend, Mrs. E. D. Poe, of Roanoke, Virginia, for her counsel; to Mrs. William McMurry for encouraging and advising me; and to the missionaries mentioned for permission to relate their experiences.

My prayer is that all readers will become so transparent before the Lord that he can hear their prayers for such a quickening in our American churches as will result in the knowledge of the Saviour being sent to a lost world.

BERTHA SMITH

Contents

1

In the Lord's School

Eight years after volunteering for foreign mission work, I was appointed to work in China by the Foreign Mission Board of the Southern Baptist Convention, July 3, 1917. I arrived in Shanghai, September 4.

Although my four years in college, two of teaching, and two in seminary were preparation for the work, I found that the most important lessons had to be learned after reaching the field.

Loneliness

Lo, I am with you alway. Matthew 28:20

The first year was spent in Peking, studying the language with other young people in the College of Chinese Studies, where all was new and interesting. I then went to live in Laichowfu, Shantung, which was four days' travel from the port of Chefoo by mule litter—speed limit three miles per hour! And I assure you that it was never broken!

I was the eighth missionary there. The youngest of the others was forty years old. I was still in my twenties and then did not know any better than to think that she was an old woman.

I continued language study with a private teacher five hours a day, and in addition taught a few English classes in the two mission high schools. At five o'clock I needed recreation. Those seven missionaries got their exercise walking to visit inquirers, or Christians who were sick either in body or soul. They were so given to their work that other missionaries called them "the devotees."

Being assured that it would be safe to walk alone in the fields from five o'clock to six each day, if I kept in sight of our mission building, I started out walking the paths that surrounded the tiny farms. I was just lonesome and homesick enough to die. Needless to say, I lost my joy in the Lord and became sorry for myself (a poor subject for any woman to get on her mind).

One day I came to myself and talked to the Lord like this: "I did not come to China of my own accord. In your Word you say that when we go to tell people about you, you go with us, even unto the end of the age. Now the end of the age has not come, so this promise includes today, right now!" And when I began to praise him for his presence, he was there.

Language was studied with a new zest. Drilling on the pronunciation of English words was no longer a burden, for my Lord was in the room with me, enabling me and helping the Chinese students. And what a joy to have an hour alone with my Lord in the fields where I talked aloud with him, even though some Chinese occasionally walked up behind me and probably thought that I was out of my mind. I not only talked with the Lord, I wanted him to talk with me; so I carried my New Testament and memorized many choice verses, stopping long enough to read one and then to repeat it over and over to the Lord as I walked.

Fortunately, as a child I had done a great deal of memory work in both Sunday school and public school. In those days, most public schools had morning worship, and Scripture passages were assigned for memory work. Later, when I was a freshman in Winthrop College, I memorized 615 Bible verses. Miss Helen Miller Gould made this assignment, for which she gave a nice leather-bound Bible. Now, all these passages came to life as I repeated them to the Lord day after day in my walks.

Sometimes I took a hymnbook and learned hymns in the same way, changing the third personal pronouns to the second, so that instead of singing *about* the Lord, I sang *to* him.

Through the years I have never had another lonely moment on land, sea, or in the air, neither have I ever had quite enough time to be alone with the Lord.

My Covenant

As soon as Zion travailed, she brought forth her children. Isaiah 66:8

One of my first China heartaches was in seeing a land where there was no observance of the Lord's Day. I could not get accustomed to all the shops being open and people going on with their field work. When the missionaries did not buy from the street vendors, they would ask, "Is it Sunday?"

Even worse were the sights on the big market and temple days. The crowds came from every direction, bringing their wares for sale. The grandmothers and children came along to go to the temple to worship. The offering of a bolt of flowered paper or silk, according to the financial status of the family, was first burned in the big pot in the courtyard. Then the worshipers walked up steep rickety stairs and bumped their foreheads on the floor before a dumb idol.

High school students stood in the courtyard and laughed at what they called the superstition of their own mothers and grandmothers who still believed in gods. In the city government high school, 398 of the 400 students were members of what they called "The No-God Society." Of the twenty teachers, all but two were members of that same society. They were just as lost as were the ardent idol-worshiping grandmothers, the mercenary men, and the wives and sisters at home. All were "as sheep without a shepherd." My heart was made sick over them, as I knew that their only hope was in coming to know my living Lord.

I had been convinced that it was not the Lord's will for me to marry. Up until my second year in China, I had thought that I would be content to live single. How little did I realize what I was saying when I sang so sincerely, "I Surrender All." The Lord gave me a mother heart, the depth of which I had not fathomed, until I saw the difference in the life of a single woman and those who were living with the one whom they had chosen for a partner, and their own precious children. The married missionaries were in the will of the Lord; why could not such a life be the Lord's will for me? But these questions were answered for me in a very real and transforming experience with the Lord.

I had been in China less than two years when my father passed away in the influenza epidemic of 1918. It was necessary for me to go to Chefoo, to the nearest U.S. Consulate to sign legal papers. This meant eight days of travel there and back. I passed through one mission station going, and another returning, and stayed in the home of missionaries while in Chefoo. By the time I had started on the last stage of the journey back to Laichowfu, I had seen seven happy families with their children.

The mule litter by which I traveled was a frame of two long poles forming shafts for the mule in front and the one in the back. Ropes were laced across the middle section between the two mules. Over the ropes was a bow frame covered with a straw mat. The passenger always provided a thick quilt-like cover to fit over the mat to protect from heat in summer and cold in winter. Pillows were used, and a mattress made for the purpose was put on top of the suitcases. Sitting and lying were equally miserable.

Since mules could not be drilled in keeping step, one mule would jerk the passenger in one direction and before she got there the movement of the other mule would pull her back. At the same time, she was being shaken up and down and crosswise until she felt like the contents of a whirling washing machine.

After leaving the last mission home before reaching my station, I traveled for two days along a lonely road. Realizing what I was going back to, and that this was for life, I wept most of the first day. By the next day I knew that something had to be done.

For safety I always walked ahead of the driver of the mule litter. Local bandits sometimes needed the clothes of the traveler! For awhile I walked very fast, getting far enough ahead to stop and talk out loud. On that solitary road that ran along by the mountain range between Laiyang and Laichow-fu, I stood. Calling upon a nearby peak to be my witness, I made a covenant with the Lord:

"Lord, I want to enter into an agreement with you today. You called me to China and you gave me grace to follow in coming. I am here to win souls for you. The only thing that will take the place of my own children will be spiritual children. If you will take from my heart this pain, I will be willing to go through with just as much inconvenience, self-denial, and pain to see children born into the family of God, as is necessary for a mother to endure for children to be born in the flesh!"

In desperation I was calling upon the mighty God for help in facing the difficulties and accepting the compensations of his service, and I was not disappointed.

From that moment forward there were no more tears, for the Lord met my every heart need. I became content with my lot and began to study the Bible and books on soul-winning with a new interest. Prayer became more definite for individuals, and every opportunity to speak for the Lord was seized. The transaction has lasted until this day, and many, many times I have praised the Lord for the privilege of being a single woman with the other person's soul-need having first place in my heart.

Paul spoke of travailing in pain for the Galatians whom he had won to the Lord (4:19), and Isaiah stated that as soon as Zion travailed, sons and daughters were brought forth. When I have a heartache for a person, which can be likened to the Holy Spirit praying through me with groanings which cannot be expressed in human language, that person is soon saved. Would that I had experienced more of that kind of heart agony!

Christ, My Victory

Thanks be unto God, which always causeth us to triumph in Christ.
2 Corinthians 2:14

Before going to China I had put myself, once and for all, into God's hands, to be or to do whatever he should choose (Rom. 12:1). This decision made the way for the Holy Spirit to fill me, and when he did, Christ was enthroned in my heart and life. This infilling was a transforming experience and led me to the mission field.

In the summer of 1919, Dr. R. A. Torrey came to China to lead conferences at summer resorts. For ten days at Peitaiho I heard him speak twice a day on the work of the Holy Spirit in the life of the Christian. What a blessing! Still, not knowing how to walk in the Spirit, I was often filled today and empty tomorrow.

The next summer, Dr. Charles G. Trumbull, editor of the *Sunday School Times,* was the conference speaker, assisted by Miss Ruth Paxson, author of *Life on the Highest Plane.* Through these friends, I came into the glorious Bible truth that Christ lives in me. Joyous release! No longer did I have to strive for victory over self, the world, and the devil, but just to act on the fact that Christ was my victory and, to quote Dr. Trumbull, "Let go and let God."

When I went to Dr. Trumbull for a personal talk on how to let Christ be my victory, he called attention to the word *is* in the Bible. God, to Moses, was the ever-present God. "I am" was his name. "The Lord is the strength of my life" (Psalm 27:1). "There is therefore now no condemnation to them which are in Christ Jesus" (Rom. 8:1). "The Lord is my light and my salvation" (Psalm 27:1).

These Scripture passages so took hold of me that I realized I had been like the beggar outside the Beautiful Gate of the Temple. It was a good place for the man to beg, but he was still helpless. After Peter took his hand, and the Lord healed him, he ran, jumped, and even rushed into the Temple praising God (Acts 3).

When I saw the glorious truth that the Lord *was* at that very moment my victory over every sin, over every disposition, and over every circumstance, I was filled with thanksgiving. When I had praised the Lord, Dr. Trumbull wrote in his notebook by my name the words, "A five-thousand-dollar gift!" But that did not half express it. I so walked on air that it was a year before I was convicted of an old sin, and how brokenhearted I was then!

Sometime afterwards I made a special study of 2 Corinthians 9:8. For two weeks I used the one verse at a Christians' Bible class, taking one word each day.

God.—The living, all-knowing, all-loving, ever-present **One** deserved my constant adoration and worship.

Is.—God here and now *is* all that he ever has been!

Able.—He is the all-powerful One who spoke the universe into existence. Certainly he is *able* to do for me all that I can ever need.

To make.—God, having created all from nothing, can make that which does not exist in order to supply my need. He "calleth those things which be not as though they were" (Rom. 4:17). He will make all things work together for my good (Rom. 8:28).

All grace.—That which is the favor of God; I cannot by any effort merit it. It being God's free gift, I can only accept it. God gives not just enough grace for one specific need, but *all* grace, every kind of loving favor sufficient for every situation.

Abound.—There would not be just enough strength, wisdom, and patience to get by, but abundance which could never give out.

Toward you.—To whom? "God is able to make all grace abound *toward you*," which means *me!* Regardless of any lack I may have in natural ability and gifts, that grace abounds toward me. I can take it according to my need.

To every good work.—Why is such abundant grace given to me? Is it that I sometimes may do a little service for him?

It is that I may *always* serve him! How? Am I just to serve
in my own human weakness? No! I, "always having all suf-
ficiency in all *things,* may abound to every good work."

What a sentence! You may be sure that by the time that I
had worked on this verse for two weeks, it had come alive for
me. Such a victorious, abundant life should only be the normal
life for one in whom Christ himself was actually living his
own life. Shame on me that at times afterwards I forgot that
magnificent truth!

However, when I recalled and acted upon it, the Lord was
there meeting every need. Dr. Trumbull taught us to sing, not
"I Need Thee Every Hour," but "I Have Thee Every Hour."
Oh, "I have Thee," and what a difference!

One Presbyterian minister at the conference said in his
testimony, "I'll have to change my whole praying vocabulary."
Yes, he would be thanking the Lord for all that he already
was to him, instead of begging him to become this or that.

Truly, life for many of us was to be on a higher plane.
Later, when I had to go through bombings and shellings and
be responsible for standing firmly before the Japanese soldiers,
what the Chinese friends called courage was not just courage.
It was Christ himself living his life in me, meeting every need
in his abounding way.

This precious truth, that Christ lives his life in us, became
especially valuable through the years when it was necessary
for me to rebuke sin. Because Christ was living in me and
being permitted to express himself through me, I could reprove without a thought of what the consequences might be
toward me personally.

Nerves

When he giveth quietness, who then can make trouble? Job 34:29

Winds often blew over the treeless plains of Shantung at
such a gale that I wondered if the house could take it. In addition to the winds, there were the dust storms. At midday

the sky would turn yellow, and all city shops would close. Everyone would rush home and close the doors; but even then, the fine silt would creep in at every crack and keyhole.

When I awoke in the mornings, the only white place on the bed would be that portion of the pillow protected by my head. These dust storms usually lasted for three days, and only the sustaining presence of the Lord enabled me to endure them.

One evening the wind was raging at bedtime. My Old Testament reading was in Psalm 127, and a statement jumped up from the page into my heart, "He giveth his beloved sleep" (v. 2). I said, "Thank you, Lord. I am your beloved because you see me in your beloved Son, so I take sleep from you." In a moment I was sound asleep until morning, even though the wind raged on through the night. From this experience I learned to take peace from the Lord during the varied storms that arose in the work.

The saintly missionary, Blanche Rose Walker, who lived in a little Chinese house alone, was having thirteen guests for meals during a convention. In writing to me about it, she added, "The Lord is holding on to my nerves." I said, "Surely, Lord, you are the one to hold on to a woman's nerves, for she can't hold them herself." I turned mine over to him and he has held them ever since.

Satisfied

While I live will I praise the Lord. Psalm 146:2

After completing my first two years of language study, I took charge of the girls' boarding school. I was able to teach some Bible in Chinese, in addition to my English classes. However, when I observed one of my teachers in the trigonometry class, I scarcely would have known if he had held the book upside down. But further work on the language was continued with a teacher three hours a day for the next five years, until furlough time.

The missionary's term of service in China was seven years for the first term, and nine afterwards. So many people went to heaven, instead of back home to America, before the nine years were up, that the term was cut to seven years. My second seven years, I studied two hours a day with a teacher; and my third seven, I had a teacher come twice a week for two hours at a sitting.

While in charge of the school, I felt I was doing the greatest work in the world. Girls came in from country villages over five counties. Some came from Christian homes, others came from non-Christian homes where some man of the family clan had been "outside" to a port and returned wanting the girls of the family educated. Often a student became the first Christian in her village, and her home became a place for a Bible woman or missionary to gather in the neighbors and tell them about the Saviour. Some of the girls became teachers or nurses, and a few of them full-time church workers. But most of them became Christian homemakers.

The greatest privilege of my first ten years was that of living with the saintly Miss Alice Huey, of Alabama. Dr. Jeannette Beall would say, teasingly, "Huey is of the heavens, heavenly; Bertha is of the earth, earthy." The mission built a house for us beside the school, and I was able, with personal money from home, to buy enough land for us to have a yard in grass, a vegetable garden, and plenty of flowers.

A gardener who loved every leaf that grew was secured for three or four dollars a month. After eating from that wage, he bought a little land each year. Although he was present for our household worship at six each morning and heard the Word in his own language, it took an object lesson to stop him from working on Sunday.

One Sunday upon returning from an afternoon Sunday school, I found the yard with rows of seedlings freshly set out. When I went out the next morning and pulled up every one and asked him to reset them, he was cured.

A pair of scissors was kept by the front door, and when we

escorted guests to the outside gate, a bunch of flowers was cut for them. Non-Christians often came just to see the flowers, and no doubt the flowers made a good impression for the Lord.

Sometimes as I thrilled over the beauty of the flowers and rejoiced because of conviction for sin in the heart of a new girl, or the growth in grace of those who loved the study of the Word, the Holy Spirit would whisper to my heart, "Would you be willing to leave your home here and the school which you so love, and go to the new work in the Western part of the province?" I always answered, "Yes, Lord, if that is what you want!"

2

A
New
Thing

When I reached North China, I found missionaries grieved over the lack of spiritual fervor on the part of most church members. In every mission station leaders were praying for an awakening. As the years went by, the missionaries began to fear that many of the church members had accepted Christianity in their minds without having been born of the Spirit.

Longing for Revival

If I regard iniquity in my heart, the Lord will not hear me. Psalm 66:18

After Dr. Trumbull's Victorious Life Conference in 1920, when some of the members of my station were blessed, missionaries and Chinese leaders set aside the first day of each month, regardless of the day of the week, as prayer day for revival. Some stayed at the church from nine to twelve o'clock and from two to five just to pray. Others went whenever they could. A different leader directed the praying each hour.

This schedule was followed for several years, and though we saw more blessings upon the work, we did not see the revival for which we had longed and prayed. In March, 1927, when the southern revolutionary army burned Nanking, the American Consul in Chefoo telegraphed missionaries: "Proceed to the coast at once." Those on the south side of the peninsula and in the western part of the province went to Tsingtau, while those on the north side went to Chefoo.

Twenty-seven missionaries, both spinsters and couples with children, plus their dogs, packed into two mission residences in Chefoo. Humanly speaking it would have been a difficult time indeed, but we had the Lord!

The "Red" influence in the army at that time led the soldiers to ridicule churches and persecute Christians. In a city in Hunan in a street parade, an old beggar man in rags was labeled "God the Father," a donkey was labeled "Jesus," and an ox, the "Holy Spirit."

Longing for our Christians in Shantung to stand true if persecution should reach them, we in Chefoo began to meet for an hour every morning after breakfast to pray for them. Soon we were praying until midday but no one remembered to pray for the Chinese Christians. All were beseeching the Lord to show *us* what he had in mind to teach *us* by permitting us to be torn from the work which we loved more than our own lives, and to be packed up in the port city.

As the days passed, we asked Jane Lide to give some Bible messages on a subject, "Christ, Our Life," which had recently become very precious to her. The Holy Spirit used the Word, as she presented it, to give each of us a clearer look at ourselves and at the all-sufficient Christ who was wanting to live his life in us all the time!

While we were weak, he wanted to be strength in us.

While we were stupid, he wanted to be wisdom in us.

While we were sinful, he wanted to be holiness in us.

While we were easily aroused and intolerant, he wanted to be patience in us.

While we were proud of the talents which he had given us— the education which he had made possible, of the experiences through the years which he had guarded, and even of "our work" which we had been able to accomplish for him—he wanted us to die to self and let him be our humility. If in any respect we were unwilling to go all the way with the Lord, he himself would be willingness in us.

Needless to say, as we dug into the Word along these lines, we were convicted of sin, enriched in our lives, and stirred with a deepened desire for revival in the Chinese churches.

Missionaries from several North China provinces were refugeeing in Chefoo at that time. Among them was Miss Marie

Monsen, an Evangelical Lutheran from Norway. We heard how she had been used of the Lord for twenty-five years in Bible teaching and evangelistic work and in seeing the sick healed. Consequently, we invited her to meet with us in our prayer meetings.

While she did not ordinarily mention the healings, upon request she shared with us some of the experiences of seeing the sick healed by the Lord.

One of our number, Mrs. Charles Culpepper, Sr., had suffered much from optical neuritis, which had left only partial vision in the eye affected. A few months before we were called to Chefoo, the good eye began to cause trouble. The mission doctor in Laichowfu advised her to go to Peking for treatment.

The Culpepper family went to Union Medical College Hospital. Due to the philanthropy of John D. Rockefeller, Jr., the world's best specialists were to be found there. The eye specialist at that time was from Vienna, Austria. He changed her glasses but gave no encouragement about an improvement in the general condition of her eyes.

During those days in Chefoo when we often had fellowship with Miss Monsen and heard her tell how God had marvelously healed all sorts of diseases, Mrs. Culpepper started having eye trouble again. There was still no eye specialist nearer than Peking, which was over 200 miles away. She did not believe he could do much for her, even if she could receive his care. She truly felt discouraged.

One evening the thought came to her to ask Miss Monsen and the prayer group to pray that the Lord would heal her. It was a very difficult thing to bring herself to do, for she still had the prejudice which had been in her mind for years concerning faith healing. But, reassured by her husband, they went together to speak to Miss Monsen about it.

By that time some of the refugeeing missionaries had returned to the United States, leaving eighteen of us. Some of them said that miracles of bodily healing were granted to first-century Christians as a proof that Jesus had risen from the dead. Now that the New Testament was completed, God expects people to believe the written record. Others said, "My God shall supply every need of yours." Certainly this was a definite need with no human remedy.

Since praying for the sick to be divinely healed had never been in her way of belief or practice, Mrs. Culpepper had never studied the Bible from this viewpoint. It was really the work of the Spirit during those days that brought her life before her like a movie. She began to see her real self as God saw her. Only the power of the Holy Spirit could have given her strength to talk very frankly with her husband, confessing sins against him and others. Even greater courage was given her to say to the whole group that she was most unworthy to be one of their number.

She was not the only one who was getting altogether right with God during that week. All of us who expected to pray for the eye were doing deep heart-searching. We were calling upon the Holy Spirit, who is Light, to shine into the deep recesses of our beings, to reveal anything that he was ready to prune out at that stage of our Christian development.

When the day agreed on arrived, twelve were present in the prayer meeting. Dr. Culpepper read from the fifth chapter of James. He did not try to explain it; he was not leaving out anything of which the Bible spoke. He then put some olive oil on Mrs. Culpepper's head and asked all to come up and lay their hands on her head and pray.

I had gone into that room, so far as I knew, absolutely right with the Lord. I would not have dared to go otherwise. But when I stretched my hand out to Mrs. Culpepper's head, I had to bring it back. There stood facing me a missionary with whom there had been a little trouble. In her early years she had been head of a girls' school, but for several years she had been teaching illiterate women to read.

I had been asked to serve as principal in our boys' school in Chefoo while the missionary principal was on furlough. I had majored in education, and by that time had had ten years' experience in teaching and thought that I was "the last word" in education! I had recommended Miss Hartwell to lead daily worship in that school. After a few weeks, I asked another missionary to tell her that methods for teaching old women were not appropriate for high school boys. She was hurt, of course.

But what about my proud self? I did not have a particle of sympathy for her. Right there before everyone, I had to say, "Miss Hartwell, I did not have the proper attitude toward you about that school affair. I beg you to forgive me!" My hand then joined the others and we prayed.

Had I refused to confess that sin, and joined in the prayer with it covered, I believe that I would have hindered the prayer of the others, and the eye could not have been healed.

Because all were right with God and of one heart, heaven came down! We did not have to wait to see whether or not Mrs. Culpepper's eye was healed! We knew in our hearts that she would never have another attack. The Lord had heard the prayers of such human frailty and had performed a miracle in healing one whom we so loved! She did not put her glasses back on. While the sight was not restored completely in the weak eye, both were strengthened and not once has she had any more pain, though using her eyes steadily for reading and needlework.

Walking around the room rejoicing and praising the Lord, we were all on a mountaintop of ecstasy. Then I had to be the joy-killer. There came over me such a sense of our inconsistency, that I had to speak of it.

"What kind of missionaries are we?" I asked. "We have gone through a week of heart-searching, humbling ourselves before each other and before the Lord, in order that we might be altogether right with him, so that he could hear our prayers and heal the physical eye of one of our own number. Yet we have never gone to this much self-negation for preparation to pray for the opening of the spiritual eyes of the Chinese to whom we have been sent." Our mountaintop of ecstasy suddenly became a valley of humiliation. We all went to our knees in contrite confession for having been so careless as to have gone along supposing that we were right with the Lord, while holding all kinds of attitudes which could have kept the Lord's living water from flowing through us to the Chinese.

Within a few weeks we were able to return to our various posts of work. Everyone went back teaching and preaching the tragedy of sin in the life and heart of a Christian. First our preachers and Bible women were convicted of sin, and then the teachers in our mission schools and other church leaders began to see themselves.

One evening as I went into the schoolyard, one of the Chinese teachers asked to see me. When we went into my office and I started to light the lamp, she said, "Please do not make a light. I cannot look into your face and make this confession!" Sitting there in the dark, she suggested that she bring her high school diploma back to me because she had cheated on one of her examinations. Knowing that the Lord was dealing with her, I had to tell her to bring the diploma back. I would not be willing for her to keep it under those conditions with my name on it.

I kept the diploma with my precious things until the Japanese occupied my house and relieved me of all my valuables and invaluables.

Later, that teacher, who had gotten right with the Lord at such a price, was able to hear the call of the Lord to other work. She resigned from the school, attended our North China seminary for three years, and became one of our most effective Bible teachers.

The pastor of our city church remarked that he had been like a fireplace with wood all laid but no match struck. When he got all known sin out of his heart and let the Lord reveal to him the unknown, the fire blazed.

Some of the missionaries who were refugeeing in Tsingtau came in contact with one who was preaching on the "Fullness of the Holy Spirit." Pearl Caldwell began in earnest heart-searching and deep humility to seek all that the Lord had for her, and was literally filled to overflowing. When she returned to Pingtu she began majoring in her teaching on the *power of the Holy Spirit* as shown in the Acts of the Apostles, and soon the preachers on the Pingtu field began to hunger for what they saw in her.

Miss Marie Monsen

Let every thing that hath breath praise the Lord. Psalm 150:6

After the healing of Mrs. Culpepper's eyes, the missionaries of Hwanghsien recommended Miss Monsen to their city church for a two-week meeting. The Chinese church invited her for the following spring, without knowing anything of her message or of her methods. They did not want to miss anything which the missionaries thought would be a blessing.

When Miss Monsen was packing to go from Tientsin over to the port of Hwanghsien, the Holy Spirit kept suggesting to her that she should buy some apples. The voyage over was only one night, but since the voice was insistent, she bought a basket of apples, thinking that someone might be sick and need them. She also took a box of chocolates, which someone had sent to her for Christmas.

Her steamer was taken over by twenty pirates, and for days she had an apple a day and a few chocolates. By the time the chocolates were eaten, food came from another source: the second mate, who had a box of eggs hidden in Miss Monsen's compartment, began sharing these with her. At two o'clock in the morning, he would slip four of the eggs down to the galley, boil two for himself and two for her, then sneak them back to her while the pirates were asleep.

When Miss Monsen returned thanks, she asked the Lord to make the eggs take the place of meat, bread, vegetables, and every vitamin that she needed. She would not eat the food served to her by the pirates since it all was stolen loot.

She not only had food to eat, but Miss Monsen virtually became the captain of the ship. Of the two hundred passengers and thirty-five crew members she was the only one who was not put into the hold. Her small compartment had only a wooden shelf for a bed. She had taken no bedding, but as she sat on her "shelf" and quoted the promises of God, it became her "throne." She gave orders to the pirate chief to give air to the passengers below, to keep the deck washed clean, and to be responsible for seeing that the dozen women passengers were not molested.

Time and time again the pirates planned to take her off the steamer and hold her for ransom. She calmly quoted the Lord's promises and trusted him not to let her be taken off.

Through the entire province of Shantung her testimony spread as to how the Lord kept her heart and mind in peace, provided the necessary food, and saved her from harm at the hands of the wicked opium fiends. As a result, all of the churches of the province wanted her to come for meetings.

During the first years of her missionary career, Miss Monsen's main work was that of teaching the Bible to church members. After fourteen years of this work, she reached the conclusion that most of the members had been convinced of the truth in their minds, without having been born of the Spirit. She would quietly say, "Dead people cannot eat!"

Believing that "the love of Calvary could not be appreciated until the people had heard the thunder of Sinai," it became her custom, at one service a day, to hold up God's holy standard for man. At the other daily service, she dealt with specific sins. The time between the two services she spent in prayer for the Holy Spirit to use the Word to bring conviction for sin to the hearts of her hearers.

Standing by the church door at the close of the services, she would take the hand of each one and look straight into his eye and ask, "Have you been born of the Spirit?" If he answered in the affirmative, the next question would be, "What evidence do you have of the new birth?" When the evidence was not clear, her next statement would be, "I'm uneasy about you. Ask the Lord to show you your position before him."

We missionaries never gave comfort to anyone who became uneasy. We urged him to go make confession, and restitution where necessary, and keep praying for the Holy Spirit to continue to reveal sin.

In those days we never invited people to go forward confessing Christ as their Saviour. All of them would have gone to keep the speaker from "losing face." We dealt with them individually until they were clearly saved. Then they were assigned a class to study the meaning of church membership. Each one had an opportunity to give his testimony to the church group before being received for baptism.

It was a moving experience to see people come to us who could neither eat nor sleep nor hold their heads up because of the burden of sin. Release came when they had put their sin on Christ and made peace with everyone to whom confession was due. When Christ had been enthroned in the heart, abounding joy came.

After the meeting in Laichowfu, I went with Miss Monsen and others to Laiyang, where we had no missionaries at that time. We took the Larsons' cook to cook for the party. He had formerly been a warmhearted church member and of his own accord had conducted a Bible class for other servants.

During the meeting at Laichowfu he had become so convicted that he had no peace for days. One morning at six o'clock he appeared at my door. He had not gone to bed all night, so burdened had he been over his sins. He begged me to forgive him for having used his unclean lips to say things about me that were not true. I suggested to him that the people to whom he had said them perhaps didn't know that they were not true, so it might be well for him to go to them and make confession.

With the tears streaming, he told me what a hypocrite he had been, how blind to the sin of his own heart and life! He went to the Larsons, confessing that he had made money buying food for them on the market. He had been pocketing the difference between the market price quoted to the Larsons and the price he had actually paid. He did not know exactly how much he had stolen in that way, but offered to work two months without wages, believing that that would cover it. They agreed, since they knew the Lord was dealing with him.

The next time I saw him, after he left my home, he was in a church service. As I walked down the aisle, I was often guilty of peeping over the screen that separated the men from the women. Before taking my seat, I wanted to know how many men we had at church. This time I could see only half of that cook's face, and lo! it looked like that of an angel!

When Miss Monsen asked someone who was altogether right with God to lead in prayer, that cook arose and started off by saying, "Lord, I thank you that I am no longer I."

The missionaries went by car to Laiyang, the home town of this cook. There was not room in the car for him so he rode his bicycle and arrived the next day. The first meeting of the series was nearly over when he arrived. When Miss Monsen again asked for a brother who was right with God to lead in prayer, the cook arose and sent up such a volume of praise to the Lord that his old friends gathered around him after the service wanting to know how such a change had come over him. It was that way after each meeting. I would go on home and start the meal on that coal cookstove, knowing that the cook was worth more to those people than I could be.

Mr. Chow, an evangelist on that field, became uneasy about his own relationship to the Lord. After every service he would come to me, wanting some evidence that he was a saved man. I wanted him to produce the evidence. The last day I asked, "Mr. Chow, what are you trusting in for salvation?" Straightening himself up, he replied, "You need not tell me that after I have walked for twenty-five years over this country telling people about the Saviour, the Lord is going to turn me away from heaven's gate!" My reply was, "If that is what you are trusting in, you most certainly will be turned away!"

Miss Monsen had the custom of awaking at 2:00 A.M. to pray for the churches where she had led meetings, presenting to the Lord those who had been blessed and others who had heard the message. As she expressed it, she prayed "that those who had had the sword thrust into their hearts would have no peace until they got right with the Lord." She brought Mr. Chow to the Lord daily, and others of us who knew of his conviction prayed with her for him.

In November a year later, Mr. Larson was back in Laiyang to lead the annual workers' conference when all the preachers and Bible women from the surrounding villages gathered for a week of planning, inspiration, and Bible teaching. Mr. Larson longed for his co-workers and himself to be filled with the Holy Spirit; that was the theme of his devotional at each session.

As the days went by, that hunger increased. When the meeting closed on Wednesday night, he announced that he would remain in the church for prayer and invited others to join him. A few remained but most went to their rooms and retired.

Brother Li, pastor of the church, stayed for prayer. He could not sing at any time and for several days had been suffering with laryngitis, unable to speak above a whisper. About midnight he arose from his knees and began singing in a clear, beautiful voice. With that, Mr. Larson jumped up and exclaimed, "The Holy Spirit has come!" Suddenly both men were knocked to the floor as though struck by an electric bolt.

In a few minutes they were loudly praising the Lord while others were crying to him for mercy. The sleeping ones were aroused and rushed to the church, falling upon their knees in confession of their sins, coldness, and lack of power of the Holy Spirit in their lives. Loud hallelujahs and cries for mercy rang out through the rest of the night.

Some were convinced of not having been saved, but by daylight they had entered into the joy of the Lord. Among these was Mr. Chow, the evangelist, for whom many had been praying. He refused to take a salary for further preaching, saying that he had already accepted too much for preaching without having known the Lord or the power of the Spirit. Now and then after that he had to sell a few acres of land to get money to support his family.

Mr. Larson went back to his home in Laichowfu just in time for the workers' conference of that section. His burning testimony so moved the people that they continued in meetings through Christmas. Chinese leaders as well as missionaries so died to themselves that the Holy Spirit gloriously filled them.

In January during the Chinese New Year's vacation time, a small group of church workers and missionaries in Hwanghsien invited Mr. Larson to lead a week's prayer meeting. One by one, those attending were brought low before the Lord as the Spirit revealed what he wanted to prune from their hearts and lives. He could not fill them until they were emptied of self, and that act had to be performed by each one.

What joy the filling of the Holy Spirit brought! Martha Li, wife of one of the evangelists, walked up on the platform to give a testimony. She stood there for about two hours with the light of heaven on her face, pouring out praise to the Lord, using the words of the Psalms.

It was a humbling experience when missionaries had to confess to Chinese their lack of love and patience. When missionary and Chinese were brought low together, there was no longer any East or West.

Dr. Glass, Dr. Culpepper, Dr. Lide, and Dr. Abernathy were set on fire by the Holy Spirit. They, with Mr. Larson, were invited to church after church in Shantung, where the Lord worked mightily. They then moved into Honan Province, where a great reviving began in the churches.

Every church in Shantung felt the effects of the revival. Before it came, the attendance at our North China seminary had gotten down to three and a half students. Not that we had half a man, but one student was only half-time. The next year after the revival swept over the province, the junior college building had to be taken over for the seminary. Every year afterwards, as long as missionaries remained, there were 150 students—all that the building could accommodate—with a waiting list in every church.

While it was hard on some leaders to hear their converts declare that they had not been saved when they had previously joined the church, all rejoiced together that the Lord had done the exceeding abundant, beyond anything that we had known to ask or think. How we thrilled over seeing Christians come for an associational meeting and sit all night praising the Lord together!

Little Nina Lide ran upstairs one day and said to her mother, "Daddy is down in his study just a 'Halleluin!'"

We came to know something of what Isaac Watts meant when he prayed, "O for a thousand tongues to sing my great Redeemer's praise."

But it was not just the song of praise which thrilled everyone. When a testimony would be taken to the heart of the lost by the Holy Spirit, causing that one to break down and weep over his or her sin, we knew that we were in the midst of a mighty work of God.

Many opium fiends were saved and delivered from the binding habit. Quarreling women were transformed into loving, motherly saints, and many sick were healed and demons cast out.

Perhaps most important of all was the transformation of our Chinese preachers. When the Holy Spirit had filled them, it was amazing how the Word of God was revealed to them. Seminary teachers marveled at the riches which the poorly educated brought forth.

Many farmers became preachers. During the winter months, when unable to work because of frozen ground, they went two by two throughout sections where there were no churches, just telling what they knew of the living Lord. So many people professed to be saved that Dr. Glass, president of the seminary, and Pastor Kwan, president of the North

China Baptist Convention, made a tour through a number of villages to see about forming churches of the believers and sending some full-time preachers to them. The two men were sometimes kept up all night just reading the Word of God to the new converts.

One Chinese woman who did not know one Chinese character (word) from another, lived in such close fellowship with the Lord that she would know when he wanted to speak to her. She would go into her bedroom and sit quietly and ask, "What is it, Lord?" The Holy Spirit would then give her a chorus of praise with a tune. When she had been given three hundred of these, a preacher visited her village and wrote them down—both words and tune—from hearing her sing them. They were printed and sung all over North China.

A Great Surprise

Marvel not that I said unto thee, Ye must be born again. John 3:7

After Lucy Wright had been a faithful, hard-working missionary nurse for nine years, I received, on an October day, a most surprising letter from her. She was so filled with the joy of the Lord that she had to share the good news with me. The day before, she had been born into the family of God!

Lucy was a most lovable, charming person, guarded in her remarks about others, easy to live with, and in every respect delightful. However, something which I had not been able to understand was that I had not had the oneness of spirit with her that I did with other missionaries. There seemed a barrier between us.

Of course, I rejoiced that Lucy was happy in the Lord but did not agree with her that she had just been saved. I surmised that her new uplift from the Lord was so wonderful that she was underestimating all of her former experiences with him. In my reply to her letter I avoided the terms, "born again" and "saved," only expressing my joy that she had been so blessed and was rejoicing in the Lord.

Our mission stations were sixty miles apart, which meant that I saw Lucy only once a year at our mission meeting. At that time all of the single women got kissed! The following summer when I arrived in Chefoo for mission meeting and all the ladies came out to meet me with that annual greeting, Lucy among them, that "wall" between Lucy and me was gone. I felt the same spiritual kinship with her that I did with the others.

At five o'clock the first afternoon of mission meeting, I asked Lucy Wright to go with me for a walk. My first sentence to her was, "Lucy, tell me why you thought that you had not been saved until last October?" She told me the following experience.

The autumn before, when Miss Monsen was in Lucy's station leading meetings, Miss Monsen had requested all of the missionaries to ask each person whom they met whether or not he or she had been born again. If they got an answer in the affirmative, they were to ask what evidence they had of the second birth. Lucy, wanting to co-operate, tried to ask that question of one woman after the morning meeting.

To her amazement, as she asked this question she had a strangling feeling and the suggestion, "You are not born again yourself. How dare you ask that question of another?" Although she tried again and again through the day, that question stuck in her throat before each person.

In utter amazement she asked herself, "What does this mean? Can it be that I myself have not been born of the Spirit?" So uneasy did she become that for two days she sought assurance in her former works of churchgoing, Bible study, tithing, singing, Sunday observance, and so on. But all to no avail. Then the third night she got on her knees alone before the Lord and prayed, "Lord, show me my condition before thee!" The faithful Lord, knowing the sincerity of her soul, brought before her the sins of a lifetime and revealed something of the exceeding sinfulness of her own heart.

For the first time, Lucy saw the meaning of Calvary. When

she had taken refuge in the death of Christ, she became conscious of a cleansing and was filled with the joy of the Lord. For the first time, she came into personal relationship with God.

As Lucy shared with me some of the attitudes of her past, I knew that she could not formerly have been a child of God. When she was twelve years old, the other girls of her Sunday school class joined the church. They and the teacher wanted Lucy to join. She did so, partly to please them and partly because she thought that being baptized would make her a Christian.

When I asked why she went to the mission field, she stated that it was a result of having felt that service was what God expected of Christians. Since her father and younger brother were physicians and surgeons, her choice of nursing as a profession seemed the natural thing to do.

In church and college she heard of the need for missionaries in China. Through her nurses' graduation sermon, she felt God was leading her to go there as a nurse. The subject was "China's Need for Christian Nurses"; the text: "Who knoweth whether thou art come to the kingdom for such a time as this?" The leading was clear, and after more than a year's resisting it, she gave in at a student volunteer meeting.

What a soul-winner Lucy Wright became after having been born of the Spirit!

3

Continuing
Revival

Revival fires continued to burn. Earnest prayer and witnessing, with daily confession of sin, kept missionaries and Chinese
Christians aglow. The Lord sent other co-workers whom he
used to fan the fires of holy zeal into a mighty flame.

Dr. John Sung
If ye shall ask . . . I will do. John 14:14

Dr. Sung, who became known as the Billy Sunday of China,
was the oldest of twelve children. His father was a preacher
and his mother was a woman of prayer, both products of old-
time Methodist mission work.

When John Sung finished high school he was sent to the
United States to a state university to study. His father hoped
that John would prepare to teach and later help send the other
brothers and sisters to the United States to study.

During his first year in America John was faithful in church
attendance and was very interested in the Y.M.C.A. work on
the campus. In his second year he was made president of the
college Y.M.C.A. and was active in all forms of Christian work.
But in his third year he lost interest in his church and even refused to serve when again elected president of the Y.M.C.A.

In his fourth year John seldom went to the Y.M.C.A. meetings and never attended church on Sunday. After he had studied three more years under "American heathens" he did not
believe anything that his parents had taught him.

In the meantime, the brother next to John came to the same
university. In true "big brother" style, John made him black
his shoes, do his laundry, and act as servant in general.

When John received the Doctor of Philosophy degree and became "Dr. Sung," he was ready to return to teach in the University of Peking. Then he became disturbed indeed over having departed from all that his godly parents believed. How could he face them? The nearer the time came to go back, the more miserable he became. Finally he decided to remain in the United States a year longer and attend a seminary. From his own study of the Bible he would decide whether his parents and the missionaries were right, or his university professors.

Dr. Sung chose what he supposed to be the best theological seminary in America, but to his amazement he soon found that his professors, though brilliant men and delightful teachers, did not accept the Bible as the Word of God and a true record of God's dealings with man. In spite of this shock, he continued his study with deep interest, and evidently his teachers delighted in the brilliant student. One of them assigned him a seat in the choir of the church which he pastored (even though Dr. Sung could not sing), so he would be able to hear the sermon without waiting in a long line to get only standing room.

That trained scientific mind had not been studying the Bible many months until he saw that Jesus Christ was either God come in the flesh to die for man's sin, or he was the greatest imposter that the world had ever known.

The more clearly he saw the truth, the more miserable he became over his own sin and failure in the sight of holy God. One day when he could stand the burden no longer, he got on his knees in his room and prayed, "Lord, I believe that you are God come in the flesh, and you came to die for my sins! I put my sins and my sinful self upon you! Come into my heart and be my Lord!" The Lord did just what he had asked him to do, and Dr. Sung jumped up and went running down the hall, praising the Lord and telling the fellows that he had been saved.

When he went to class praising the Lord, teachers were as amazed as fellow students had been. Dr. Sung became so heartbroken over both students and faculty that he could only plead with them to turn to the Saviour. They thought that he had lost his mind and had him sent to an insane asylum!

He would say to the psychiatrist, "I am not crazy! I have just been reborn. My soul which has been in misery is filled with the joy of the Lord and I cannot but praise him!" But since the faculty of the seminary had sent Dr. Sung there, the psychiatrist did not release him, although they found no reason for his being kept.

He spent 193 days in the institution, just reading the Bible all day long. He was soon convinced that what China most needed was not science teachers but preachers of the gospel, and that he must give his life to telling people about his Saviour.

Some furloughed missionaries from Korea heard of Dr. Sung and requested his release, promising to return him to the institution upon any sign of insanity.

Finally he was on his way back to China. Fearing that his family would overpersuade him to teach, he got out his diplomas and threw them into the Pacific Ocean. He would have no evidence that he had passed his examinations and was qualified to be a teacher.

Upon reaching his country, he first went home to praise the Lord with his parents, and then arranged to marry the girl to whom he had been engaged since childhood. He allied himself with the Bethel Bible School of Shanghai and became the school's field evangelist. He was joined by six of the Bible School graduates, who formed the "Bethel Band" which went all over China preaching and singing the gospel.

The Chinese high regard for education led the best-educated people to hear Dr. Sung. The fact that his Ph.D. was in science especially attracted the educated, for they had been under the impression that science and the Bible did not agree. They not only came, but, due to the fascinating way that sin and the Saviour were presented in the power of the Holy Spirit, they came forward confessing their sin and their desire for Christ.

All the space at the front of the building and down the aisles was filled with the kneeling, whose tears of repentance left wet spots on the floor.

With Dr. Sung, following Christ was not made easy. Wrongs must be made right insofar as possible. After a two-week campaign in Peking, twenty thousand dollars were paid back in old debts or wrongfully gained money.

In our Shantung churches so many debts were so old that the person to whom the money was due was either not living or could not be located. When the "conscience money" was brought to the churches, the brethren announced that the Lord did not want that kind of money in his treasury. It was used to create a fund for beggars.

One day Dr. Glass was kneeling near the long-time treasurer of the large city church at a prayer meeting. Suddenly the treasurer cried out, "Lord, have mercy on me! I've stolen! I'm a thief! I have stolen from God!"

In astonishment Dr. Glass said to himself, "Not you, Brother Wang; surely not you! All these years you have been such a trustworthy, devoted deacon, faithful trustee of the seminary, and upright Christian gentleman. You just could not have taken money from the church treasury!"

After a while Brother Wang got control of himself enough to say, "I have not paid my tithe to the Lord! According to his Word, I have stolen it from him!"

No doubt Brother Wang had thought himself a liberal giver. He was not content to turn over a new leaf and begin tithing. He had an old debt which he wanted paid. He would pay any price in order to be altogether right with God.

Fortunately, Chinese keep accurate household and personal accounts. Brother Wang counted up his tithe from the time he became a Christian, more than twenty years before, subtracted from it the total amount contributed to the church, and had left such a debt that he had to sell some land in order to pay it. What a flame he became for the Lord after getting altogether right with him!

Dr. C. W. Pruitt said of Dr. Sung, "No living man has given up more for the gospel!"

With him, every moment besides that necessary for personal care was spent preaching, praying, preparing his messages, or engaging in personal interviews. Little interest was shown in any subject except as it related to his Lord. Then he was all attention.

Before Dr. Sung's meetings in Tsining, the missionaries had been praying for Dr. Hou, who had been educated in a mission school. He not only had quit going to church, but also had been ridiculing those who did go.

From the first service, Dr. Hou was there to hear the scientist. We missionaries watched his face day by day, as first he showed interest, then concern, and, after a few more days, misery. Imagine our thrill as we saw him go down the aisle and get on his knees, acknowledging himself a lost sinner in need of the Saviour.

At the close of the meetings, he volunteered to be the leader of one of the twenty-four evangelistic bands which had been organized. He became concerned about a church six miles from the city. Not having a leader, the members had grown so cold that not only would no one lead services, but they had quit meeting together. They had even stored their harvested crops in the little church building.

Dr. Hou left his drugstore and clinic and, with the pastor of the city church and a spirit-filled church member, went out to the little church to stay a few days. The people came to hear them.

Dr. Hou led the first service, giving his personal testimony to the change the Lord had wrought in his heart. For three days the three men testified, prayed, and preached until late at night, longing for the Holy Spirit to come in transforming power. By the last day people had become so heart-hungry for the gospel that they were willing to come by way of repentance and confession of sin, and more people who were dead in sin were brought to life.

That new group formed a witnessing band of fifteen members. Without a preacher, church services were started again and a Bible class was held each evening where twenty met to study.

Another interesting convert during Dr. Sung's meeting in my church, was a young teacher who was the twenty-seventh child of his mother. She said that she would have had a real family, had not her husband died when number twenty-seven was a baby. I supposed that it was just as well that the first twenty-five did not live, since the boy and girl who were left, came near starving.

The boy was sent to a mission school and one day, while standing to recite, fainted. Upon investigation, the teacher found that he had not had a bite to eat in three days. He was such a bright and promising student that a missionary paid his expenses through high school and university. While at the university, he gave up his belief in Christianity.

When we saw him go forward and kneel in response to Dr. Sung's message, we knew that another miracle was taking place.

When prayer centered on another doctor, we expected something to happen again, even though he was a slave to a bad disposition, cigarettes, and opium. After a few days of hearing the gospel he was saved and instantly delivered from every unholy habit. His testimony and his daily presence at the evening Bible class thrilled us for months, and when he became a deacon and one of our strongest leaders, we were filled with praise to our God.

Recognizing Dr. Sung to be a man of power in prayer, Christians with physical ills began coming to him for prayer for healing. He gave the Word of God and prayed for their healing, only after he was convinced that they wanted health in order to serve the Lord more effectively. The Lord honored the prayer of faith and many were thus healed.

Joseph, son of Deacon Chiang, developed tuberculosis of the bone in a lower limb, when six or seven years old. He spent years in the children's ward of the mission hospital in Lai-chowfu, where he was loved and tenderly cared for by Dr. Jeannette Beall and Alda Grayson, superintendent of nurses, and their staff.

When Joseph was about fourteen, Dr. Sung was leading meetings in Pingtu. Sinners were turning to the Lord, and saints were seeing the Lord work wonders.

Mr. Chiang, Joseph's father, wrote a letter to Dr. Sung describing Joseph's condition and asking prayer for his healing. Dr. Sung read the letter to that congregation, who were in tune with the Lord. Then, laying the letter on the lectern, he put his hand on it and said, "We will all now pray in unison for the Lord to heal Joseph."

A volume of sincere prayer went up to the throne from cleansed hearts. Joseph began improving immediately; little pieces of bone worked their way out through the flesh and skin. Within another year he was working on the farm.

During the Pingtu meetings, a number of people wanting to be healed went, or were carried, to the home of the missionaries, Mr. and Mrs. Earl Parker, where Dr. Sung was staying. Among these was Mrs. Loh Kin T'ang, who had not walked since the birth of her son eighteen years previously. She was carried into the home by two men and seated on the floor. Dr. Sung kneeled down and, after praying, anointed her with olive oil. Then he commanded her in the name of Jesus Christ to rise up and walk!

Mrs. Loh got up immediately, stood for a moment, and then walked out of the home, down two sets of stone steps to the street, and upgrade for a distance of a hundred yards to the church. The song and praise portion of the service had begun. Mrs. Loh walked up on the platform and praised the Lord for having healed her.

Her husband was an English teacher in a mission school in Chefoo. When their son wrote his father of the mother's healing, every sentence of the letter included "Praise the Lord!" or "Hallelujah!"

The father was disturbed indeed. He reasoned, "This just cannot be true. My wife has spent months in the mission hospital in Pingtu, and Dr. Yocum has told me that she will never walk! My son is going off on a religious tangent!"

After another day or two, he became so concerned that he asked for a leave of absence for a week to go home and straighten out the family. The donkey-back travel would require four days to go and return, and he would need two days at home.

Chinese homes have a brick or mud wall around their yards for privacy and for protection of what they have inside. The double doors for the gate are closed from the inside with two wooden bars.

When Mr. Loh reached his gate he heard someone sweeping the yard. He called out, and the bars were slipped aside and the two doors pulled open. There stood his wife. Mr. Loh rushed inside, closed the gates behind him, and fell down on his face, confessing his sin of unbelief and coldness toward the Lord. He got up saying, "Praise the Lord! Hallelujah!" in every other sentence.

Father, mother, and son—what evangels they became, going from house to house and village to village, just bragging on Jesus! Mr. Loh gave up teaching and did full-time village evangelistic work with Pearl Caldwell and Bonnie Ray.

Soon after the healing of Mrs. Loh, Mr. Parker and Miss Caldwell were leading meetings in her home village. Mrs. Loh walked a mile to witness to Mrs. K'iao, who had not walked for twenty-eight years. After hearing what the living Lord had done for Mrs. Loh, Mrs. K'iao wanted to go to church. Expecting to go home walking, she had a pair of shoes made.

Her son carried her on his back and put her on a chair in the aisle of the crowded women's wing of the church. Men and women did not sit in the same room. The women from their wing had a side view of the preacher, without being seen by the men who sat in the main part of the church facing the speaker.

The opening part of the service took plenty of time, and Brother Parker had prepared a good message and was revived in his soul. Mrs. K'iao, having gone there to be prayed for, became impatient and kept asking, "Why doesn't he hush and let them pray for me?" Finally some of the women just knelt around her and prayed in an undertone. Since non-Christian women often talk at church, Brother Parker, accustomed to the noise, just faced the men and went on with his sermon.

When the Lord touched Mrs. K'iao's body, she got up and started home, with the shouting women following her. Some of the brethren went out to quiet them down, only to join in the loud "Hallelujahs," and before the good sermon was finished, the whole congregation—including the preacher—were in the yard and street shouting praises to God.

Mrs. K'iao walked down the main street of her village a quarter of a mile to her home, and anywhere else afterwards that she wanted to go. She was seventy-two at that time.

As in the days when Lazarus came back to life, people—including missionaries—traveled long distances just to see "Mother K'iao." Only the Lord knows how many unsaved were convinced of the truth of our living Lord and turned to him as a result of that miracle.

After a few more years Dr. Sung began in each of his campaigns to have a healing service for all who wanted to attend. Hundreds of people at these services either went or were carried down the aisle and passed by him for his prayer for healing. Without a chance to learn their spiritual state, he prayed for each to be physically healed.

Alas, the weakness of human nature! Some enlarged their infirmity in every testimony, until minor ills had become incurable diseases. Others loudly praised Dr. Sung for his power to heal. While Dr. Sung himself would have been the last to have stolen the Lord's glory, others in their enthusiasm talked of the instrument instead of the Lord himself, and our Lord would not stand for that. He will not give his glory to another.

While Dr. Sung was in his prime, he developed intestinal

tuberculosis. In spite of his own prayers and those of his many friends, he suffered agony for a number of years and died when only forty-three.

Could Dr. Sung's closing years explain why we do not now see more people definitely healed in answer to prayer?

The New Secretary Came

Which doeth great things . . . and wonders without number. Job 9:10

When revival fires had been burning in North China long enough to stir the devil into a rage, the new secretary of the Foreign Mission Board, Dr. Charles E. Maddry, came for a visit. He was accompanied by Dr. J. B. Weatherspoon, then professor of homiletics at Southern Baptist Theological Seminary. Dr. J. T. Williams, of Shanghai, went with them over China as interpreter.

Tsining was the first city in North China to be visited. They were met at the railway station twenty miles away, by Frank Connely in his car. A few hours' association with Dr. Connely would convince anyone that he was no religious fanatic.

At the supper table Dr. Maddry remarked in jest, "I hear that Katie Murray is casting out demons in the name of the Lord over in Honan Province!" I calmly replied, "Yes, we often come in contact with demon-possessed people among the Chinese. The Lord used Dr. Connely to cast out one here last Sunday!"

All eyes were on the man at the head of the table, who in a humble manner related the following:

Brother Chang, a church member from a village a few miles away, and Brother Liu, a new convert, had come to church bringing a stranger who could not speak. Brother Chang asked the pastor to request the brethren to remain after the services and pray the dumb devil out of the neighbor whom he had brought. Some of the loudest testifiers picked up their hats and went grinning toward the door as if to say, "That is too much for me."

The pastor, one old church member, and Dr. Connely went to the prayer room with the three men and got on their knees.

After each had prayed, they asked the dumb man to say, "Praise the Lord." Though trying his best, he could not get his lips open. For a week he had been in that condition, having been seized suddenly.

After having prayed for some time with the same result, Dr. Connely turned to the man and, with the voice of authority, said, "In the name of the Lord Jesus Christ, I command you dumb devil to come out of this man!" Immediately the man opened his mouth and started talking.

I then told our American visitors of how Mr. Liu, the new Christian of the group, had a few weeks previously been brought to the city by Brother Chang with the report that he was possessed by a demon that had absolute control over him. Sometimes it threw him into the water and sometimes into the fire, or anywhere else.

I was the only missionary there at the time. The Chinese pastor came asking me to go with him to lay hands on Mr. Liu and pray the devil out. I told him that I would go and pray, but that I would not lay hands on him since Jesus never put his hands on demon-possessed people. As a result of the praying, Mr. Liu was completely delivered, which led to his becoming a Christian.

Mrs. Connely told the guests of numbers of sick people who had been healed in answer to prayer.

The visitors heard similar experiences related at each mission station and listened to glowing testimonies of those who had been delivered from bondage to opium, cigarettes, wine, adultery, hatred, covetousness, selfishness, and fear of evil spirits. They saw crowds packing the churches to hear the gospel; they heard the footsteps of people making their way to the churches long before daylight, assembling for the six o'clock Bible study and prayer together; and they were told how the gospel was being carried to outlying sections of the province by "hot-hearted" laymen.

After Dr. Maddry had completed his visit of all the mission work, he held a conference in Shanghai of representatives from all the mission groups. At that conference he stated that, when traveling through Shantung and Honan provinces, he had felt that he was reliving the Acts of the Apostles.

4

Alone
upon
the
Promises

During the Depression of 1932, the executive secretary of
the Foreign Mission Board, Dr. T. B. Ray, wrote a similar letter to each of thirty-five missionaries on furlough, requesting
each to look for other work until times got better. Dr. Ray
stated that the Board was receiving only enough money to
keep on the field those missionaries who were still there. What
a blow!

A New Leading

There is no want to them that fear him. Psalm 34:9

When I received Dr. Ray's letter, I realized that I did not
have to return to China just because I had been there for fourteen years. Neither did the fact that the Board could not support me determine that I should *not* go back. Recalling how
Judah's good king, Hezekiah, took his unpleasant letter to the
Temple and spread it before the Lord, I decided to do likewise.

Five minutes' walk from my home was a little Methodist
church. It was kept open at night for men to go in and sleep
when traveling to and fro looking for work. One morning as
soon as it was light enough for the men to be gone, I arrived
at the church. Choosing a suitable prayer place, I began to
seek the Lord's will. After two months of daily meeting the
Lord there, I knew in my heart that he wanted me to return
to China.

Then came the question: How would I be able to go? In
my Old Testament daily reading I had reached Isaiah. While
turning the pages, I saw unfamiliar words, even though they

were not underscored: "I will go before thee, and make the
crooked places straight: I will break in pieces the gates of
brass, and cut in sunder the bars of iron: and I will give thee
the treasures of darkness, and hidden riches of secret places,
that thou mayest know that I, the Lord, which call thee by thy
name, am the God of Israel" (45:2-3).

"Thank you, Lord!" my heart responded. "The 'how' is the
Lord's concern. The riches are in secret. Since *he* knows, that
is sufficient."

I had to be willing to give up the privilege of working under
our Board with a group of missionaries who, to me, were the
Lord's choicest. They had their tried-and-proven mission policy, and, while advising, they left each to respect the Holy
Spirit as final guide.

I had friends who had gone out as independent missionaries
because of failure to come up to our Board's regulations in
either health or educational requirements. While I appreciated
the contribution which they were making to the cause of Christ
in China, I would never have chosen to be one of them. But I
had to get willing to go that way, or even under some other
board.

I wrote a letter to the secretary of the Foreign Mission
Board, asking for the privilege of returning to China to work
with the same relationship to the Board, to the missionaries on
the field, and to the Chinese Baptist Convention as I had formerly. The only difference now would be that I would not
receive funds from the Board for any purpose whatever. I assured Dr. Ray that I would make no appeal to any church for
funds. I asked for the privilege of working without Board support until it could take me on again. And if I could never again
be supported by the Board, I would in no way hold the Board
responsible. With this request I began to pray earnestly indeed! If the Lord wanted me to remain with the Board, he
would move Dr. Ray's heart to agree to that.

The afternoon after my letter was mailed to Dr. Ray, a friend
from Augusta Road Baptist Church, Greenville, South Caro-

lina, Mrs. C. E. Hatch, drove over to my home. She came to tell me that the Lord had revealed to her that I was to return to China. She said that at a prayer service the night before, she had been given the engagement ring of a widow, and other gifts to help send me back. She wanted to be my secretary, receiving and forwarding any funds that came in.

Dr. Ray agreed to my returning on the terms I suggested. He also offered to secure second-class passage on an American steamer across the Pacific at a missionary discount, for about $300. When I had that amount and enough to cross the continent in a day coach, with sufficient for a railroad ticket from Shanghai to North China, I praised the Lord indeed. By the time to purchase my ticket, the Sunday school of one of the churches in Spartanburg, South Carolina, had sent the amount needed for Pullman. A retired missionary in Los Angeles secured passage for me on a Danish freighter to Shanghai for $112, thus effecting a saving of nearly $200 over the original estimate for ocean travel.

Earlier in the summer I had been notified that the girls' school in East Shantung, where I had formerly worked, had been reduced, for lack of funds, to an eight-grade school. The mission decided to transfer me to the western part of the province to work with Martha Franks and Dr. and Mrs. Frank Connely. The only question in my mind concerning the transfer was what Frank Connely might think of my arriving to work on his field with no money for living or for my work. However, that, too, could be committed to the Lord.

Martha Franks wrote, "We need you. If you can secure passage money, come on back and live with me; and we will get along the best we can on my salary, going fifty-fifty with it."

Frank and Mary Connely, not knowing that Martha had written, wrote the following: "Come on back and live and eat with us. We will stretch two salaries to do for three and manage some way. You shall have everything that we do." In addition to this, Frank sent a check for one hundred dollars to help on my passage.

These factors enabled me to set sail with a light heart, knowing that a warm welcome awaited me, whether or not I had any visible funds. My traveling companion was Miss Alice Huey, whose passage and support was being provided by the Woman's Missionary Union of her home state, Alabama.

A group of praying friends accompanied us to the steamer in Los Angeles Harbor and, gathering in our stateroom, commended us to God and pled that we might be made a blessing to those on board. In response, the joy of heaven filled our souls. I usually suffer from seasickness, but I knew that on that voyage the Lord would either control the Pacific Ocean or me, for they had asked in faith that I be saved from seasickness.

Five nationalities made up the passenger list of twenty-seven. The ship, being Danish, had officers and crew from that country. I had not before seen such courtesy shown passengers.

For three months I had been asking the Lord to choose the steamer on which I was to return to China, and when I found myself among that number I knew that those were the people with whom my Heavenly Father had placed me. Miss Huey and I began to pray for all on board and to look for opportunities to speak about our Saviour.

The Lord especially laid on our hearts a lovely young Russian woman who was married to an American marine stationed in San Francisco. She was returning to Manchuria to visit her parents.

She was so full of life and fun and personal charm that it was only a few days until she was the center of interest and all aboard were calling her by her first name, Lueba. How I wanted her to know the Lord!

One cool evening as I sat alone, reveling in the beauty of a gorgeous sunset, Lueba came and nestled down beside me to keep warm. Slipping my arm into hers, I asked if she had been born from above. In quick response came one question after another, until she knew what I meant, and something new began to fill her mind.

The next day we had another long talk which revealed her heart need and, after a few days, another which showed a genuine desire to be saved. However, she was rooming with a Jewess. The roommate and another Jewess, with the latter's husband, soon had Lueba so under their influence that she feared their ridicule too much to turn to Jesus as Saviour.

The Lord's Storm

O my God, . . . make them afraid with thy storm. Psalm 83:13,15

A few days more of prayer and trust, and our God stretched forth his mighty hand in a terrific storm. It began early on December 31. During the morning, I stood in a sheltered place in the center of the back deck and, holding to the railing with both hands, looked out on both sides at what we were passing through. Never could I have imagined anything like it! My heart thrilled with the thought of the God of such power being my own loving Heavenly Father and actually living inside me!

More and more terrible the storm grew. About noon a portion of a tremendous wave struck the ship. Dishes on the dining tables went smashing to the floor. The two sideboards fell, face forward, emptying their contents of silverware and other table service. Dishes of food ready to be served slid from the galley tables and broke. Men turned white with fear , and women screamed as they were hurled across the lounge. No sooner was one such shock over than a similar one followed. Lunch was cooked three times that day. When the few who wanted to eat were finally seated in the dining saloon, another lunge caused everything to slide off the tables, while people and chairs went under the tables.

All day long and through the night, the captain remained on the bridge at the helm and the chief engineer also on duty the twenty-four hours, responding to the captain's signals for power to be turned on or off. The first officer had the responsibility of the passengers. Poor man! He looked like death itself as he went from one to another administering what today we would call tranquilizers. He saw that Miss Huey and I did not need any.

We traveled only ninety-three miles in the twenty-four hours, and that not in the direction of Shanghai.

When the first lunge of the storm came, I rushed to the lounge where most of the passengers were to see if I could help anyone. Our dear Lueba was wringing her hands and begging for someone to pray. The Jews sat helplessly around her, unable to pray or comfort. They were as frightened as she and others who were crying and praying. Well might they have been, for if one of those mountains of water, containing tens of thousands of tons, had struck the ship full force, it would have been destroyed.

I went to Lueba and, putting my arms around her, responded to her call for prayer. I was calm in the assurance that we would come to Shanghai in safety. In the name of King Jesus I lifted my voice to the God who holds the sea in his hand, and besought his comforting presence and protecting care. I assured her that we would have it until our journey's end. I was able to tell her of my own assurance that Jesus had come aboard that ship in Los Angeles, for he was living in my heart. The ship on which he traveled could not go down, not unless he willed it. She became quiet but held on to me, begging that I not leave her.

Clinging with one hand to the stationary sofa on which she lay, and holding my Bible with the other, I read to her, but loud enough so others in the lounge could also hear. I read a number of passages from God's Word, and sang one hymn after another of his peace and watchful care, until she was asleep.

Words cannot describe the feeling of my heart! It was more than assurance and rest of mind. It was joy unspeakable bubbling up and filling my soul! God the all-terrible, God the creator and controller of all the forces of nature, was in tenderest love surrounding me, his child. In fact, from his Word I knew that I was with Christ, so hidden in God that I was just as safe from the power of the angry billows as if I had been in heaven itself! All that I could do was to rejoice in it and praise him.

The three Jews and other passengers sat quietly and listened while I told them of what Jesus, God's Son and our sacrifice, came to mean to me when I laid my sins on him at the age of sixteen, and how at that very moment he was filling my heart with himself. I told them of his promise to come a second time, and that many believed it would be soon. God spoke to those Jews, Russians, Chinese, Scots, Americans, and to the Danish first officer through my words. Afterwards, we marveled and praised the Lord when a number of people told us that the expression on Miss Huey's face and mine confirmed our testimony of peace and calmness.

My lunch was sent up to the lounge. In the presence of those "good sailors" who could not eat, I praised God, who was working a miracle in me, and ate and enjoyed it all.

By midafternoon when Lueba had rested and had time to think things through, she asked me to go to her cabin with her and teach her how to pray. I explained how we come to God through Christ's death, and suggested that she pray in her own way. She so poured out her heart to God that if I had understood Russian, I would have learned something about praying from her.

A greater storm was raging in her heart than that outside. Her sins were separating her from the God whom she longed to know, and in anguish of soul she confessed and pled for deliverance. When she opened the door of her heart at which Christ had been knocking for several days, she was filled with his own peace. In the days that followed she quietly witnessed to passengers and officers, as occasions offered.

The remainder of the journey was made on calm seas under smiling skies. The first officer admitted only to Miss Huey and me that he had expected the whole deck floor to blow off, which would have meant death for us all.

When we arrived in Shanghai, I calmly walked into the American Oriental Bank and deposited the two hundred dollars which I had saved by taking the Danish freighter instead of an American passenger steamer. When I reached Tsining, which was my ultimate destination, I handed Frank Connely the check which he had sent to help on my passage. I was entering upon a new phase of my mission career (without Board support) but had money in the bank to live on for a few months.

I had a bedroom at the Connelys' home, and I fixed a little study out in their yard. I took my meals with Martha Franks. Each month without fail I was able to pay my share of the expenses.

Upon my decision to return to China that time, I had told the Lord that my food would be left with him, whether good or bad. Just about that time this verse from King Solomon's prayer leaped from the page into my heart, "Feed me with food convenient for me" (Prov. 30:8). I did not need the food of a king, neither would I be properly nourished on that of a Chinese coolie, so my food would be the right kind for me. Praise his name!

I had also told the Lord that I would not take my prayer time to beg him to supply my needs. I would go on as formerly, praying for the Chinese for whom I was responsible and leaving my bread and butter to him. Only once during the two years did I backslide in this matter.

In the second autumn when funds were getting low, I prayed for money. How ashamed I was later when I learned that gifts to our mission board had so increased that they were ready to appoint some new missionaries and would not do so without resuming support of the one on the field. The two Christmases before, many friends had sent money, but that Christmas only a little came. The Lord knew, even though I did not, that my salary would begin with January. The first year I had received the exact amount for living as the other missionaries, and the second year I had a little bonus of thirty dollars extra sent. The Lord knew that they were not having enough.

Friends spoke of my returning to China that time by faith.

To me, it was not by faith but by the living Lord. The two years without support from a mission board were no more by faith than my former years had been, when a group of men by faith had definitely planned work for the year on the basis of what the churches had given the year before.

The difference was that the gifts went to a committee or board, who would wisely divide them according to the need of each missionary, without respect to the ability of any individual to sway an American audience with his appeal. Not only was the money divided justly, according to system, but the fact that our Board was able to get ninety-three cents of every dollar to the field, meant that more actually reached the missionary than if individuals had sent their gifts directly, with all the involvements with foreign postage and exchange.

Bank Failure

My God shall supply all your need according to his riches in glory.
Philippians 4:19

During the following spring I saved up a little money for a few new summer dresses. I arrived in Chefoo for our annual mission meeting a few days early, and went to town the very next morning. I selected two pretty patterns of blue silk for dresses, wrote checks for them, then took them to a tailor.

The next day I went to town to buy other things, but when I started to write a check the clerk said, "We cannot accept that check."

Holding up my checkbook for him to see, I said, "This is a perfectly good American bank in Shanghai!"

He answered, "You just go round to the bank and exchange your check and bring us the cash."

Leaving my package, I confidently arrived at the bank, only to be informed that the American Oriental Bank in Shanghai had closed the day before. I not only had no money for that package, but had to make good the checks of the previous day.

However, I was not disturbed. I knew the Lord would straighten the matter out. Of course he did, and here is how.

Dr. Williams, our mission treasurer in Shanghai, was ready on the appointed day of the month to leave his office for the bank to deposit a month's salary for each of the Baptist missionaries in China, when a "chance" caller came in and detained him until after banking hours. The next morning the bank did not open. So Dr. Williams arrived for our mission meeting with a briefcase full of Chinese money, a month's salary for each of the North China group.

I was able to pay up my shopping bills and get back home. The two years without a salary had so completely delivered me from money that I just committed the situation to the Lord, knowing that I would get along some way until the next month.

The next day as I started with a Bible woman to visit some of the sick Christians in a hospital two miles away, I found that I did not have a dime for ricksha fare. I had to tell her why I had changed my mind about going. It was soon noised abroad that the missionary had no money.

The next morning I found only one egg on my breakfast plate. Not having American cereals or bacon, I was accustomed to eating two. When I asked the cook the reason for such economy, he replied, "Don't you know that American bank in Shanghai has failed? You can't afford to eat two eggs!"

Brother Hoh, a wheelbarrow man who had food only when he had a load to push, and who could not even afford a wife, came in to say, "I have heard that the American bank has failed, leaving you without money, not even enough for ricksha fare. I have a friend who has a ricksha, and when you want to go anywhere just let me know and I will borrow it and take you without charge." And then, looking at me with eyes full of Christian love, he added, "And I have a dollar, and if you need it you may have it!"

One of the Presbyterian missionaries had fifteen dollars which she was saving for a new afternoon dress when she would go to the port the following summer. She sent the money to me and I "ate the dress."

At Christmastime my sister sent some dress goods in her usual gift box. Among the pieces was a beautiful pea-green all-over lace. Now that Presbyterian missionary was a blonde, and what could be prettier on her than pea-green! I gave her the material, and it made for her a dress more beautiful than anything she could have secured in Tsingtau. After using it one summer, she went on furlough and sent the dress to me. I passed it on to a redheaded missionary, for whom it must have been dyed in the beginning!

So no one had been denied in order to share with me, and I had eaten two eggs.

5

Grace
for the
New
Work

When I began traveling from Tsining over a five-county area, I knew that I had been promoted. My method was first to spend a week in Bible study with the organized church in the county seat. Christians would come from all directions—one or two from a village—bringing their bedding roll on their shoulders and, in their hands, a few steamed rolls and a little jar of turnips pickled in brine. To go with this food, the church would add a drink of hot millet broth. At night the men's "beds" were spread on the brick floor of the church, while the women were "bedded down" with the pastor's wife next door.

In Country Churches
As thy days, so shall thy strength be. Deuteronomy 33:25

It was most satisfying to have a part in building up the country churches. We usually took a short New Testament book for study for the week, though sometimes I taught by subjects. In the evenings all attending classes went out on the streets, visiting from house to house, inviting the unsaved for an evangelistic message.

After the county-seat church meetings I went to the villages which had little chapels. Occasionally I was able to spend a week in a village not previously visited by a missionary. There, meetings were held on the threshing floor.

Sometimes I spent a month at a time out on these trips, never hearing a word of English except what I spoke to the Lord. Neither did I see a fire, though it might be December. The thirty pounds of clothes that I wore kept me warm during the day, and my warm bedding and hot water bottle were sufficient at night. But, oh, the transfer time from warm bed to cold room in the morning! I had to get up in time to have my own quiet hour with the Lord before the neighbors began to stir, since I was always on exhibition.

What an ordeal getting into those three suits of "long handles" down under the covers in the dark! Of course, the foot usually went a few times where the arm should go! And those eight stockings, how they twisted!

After breaking the ice to wash my face, I was awake quite enough to pray, so down the street I would go to the haystack—my prayer place.

I always let my Bible woman have the room for her praying, since my clothes were warmer than hers. My inner clothes were English wool, and my Chinese garments were wadded with silk floss, which was warmer than her cotton wadding. She didn't have a fur garment either.

Raking aside the frosted part of the hay, I would kneel down. Being the only one awake for miles around, I knew I would not be disturbed. As I looked up to the stars and worshiped and interceded, what "flavor," as my Chinese friends would say!

It was on one of these country trips that I met Mr. Pi (pronounced Be). He was the most highly educated man in his county. He had heard the preacher at the county-seat chapel preach a few times but was not impressed. One day when he took a journey of several miles by wheelbarrow, the pusher, Brother Ho, who did not know one Chinese character, told him about the Lord. Brother Ho had enough sense to memorize only one Bible verse, but he had been born of the Spirit, and he told his passenger what the Lord meant to him. The elegant gentleman scholar was definitely impressed and, upon reaching home, went several miles to the church at the county seat and purchased a New Testament. He read it and, in so doing, passed from death unto life. He said that others had talked to him about Jesus Christ, but the wheelbarrow man showed a personal acquaintance with Christ.

Just before the Japanese army entered Shantung, I was at Mr. Pi's church. Fearing that suffering might be in store for the Christians, I was trying to prepare them for it through a study of the First Epistle of Peter. One day during the study, Mr. Pi said in a prayer, "Lord, you know that I have read everything that Confucius and the other sages of China ever wrote, but never have I read anything that has the flavor of what that fisherman Peter wrote!"

Sometime afterwards, Mr. Pi was going by train to the capital of the province, Tsinan. He saw a fellow passenger in the coach whom he thought must be a Christian. He was not smoking, not restless because the train was slow and late, but was sitting in peaceful contentment. Mr. Pi thought, "If that is a Christian brother, I surely want to meet him!" But the man was handsomely dressed, and Mr. Pi was only in cotton, so he hesitated to speak.

Finally, afraid that he would miss the opportunity of coming to know a brother in the Lord, Mr. Pi thought of a plan. "Hallelujah!" he exclaimed.

The gentleman turned around, extended his hand, and said, "Oh, you are a Christian! I am, too." Together they traveled, talking of the Lord, and parted to meet again.

Village Joys

Blessed be the Lord God, . . . who only doeth wondrous things. Psalm 72:18

On an autumn day a man walked twenty-five miles to the city of Tsining to ask for someone to go to his village and tell his family and neighbors of the God whom we proclaimed. No one could go. After a few months he came again, but still no one was free. When he came the third time, I said, "I am going to that village."

Our camping outfit and food supplies were packed on a wheelbarrow, and Mrs. Han, a young Bible woman, and I went in rickshas. We started early in the morning and arrived at sunset. Most of the village were in the receiving line! The little boys were dressed in keeping with the weather, in their skins! Our enthusiasm for the greeting cooled a bit when we entered the living quarters provided for us by our host who had done the urging, and saw an ox tied at one end of the room.

I looked at Mrs. Han, and she looked at me and said, "If the King of glory could come down to this earth and be born in a stable for us, we can endure this room for ten days." I agreed with her that we most certainly could. We praised Christ that he had been born in our hearts and would enable us to endure the smell.

The room was eight feet wide, the regular width of a Chinese village home, and about ten feet long. To the right of the door, along the wall, was a narrow wooden bed-frame, with Kaffir corn stalks laced across with string. Mrs. Han put her bedding on it. The other bed ran across the end of the room. I had my camp cot but no room to put it up, except on top of that bed.

By the wall opposite Mrs. Han's bed was a little table where we were to do our cooking and eating, and beyond that stood "Mr. Ox." He could have swished his tail in the soup. If we had had soup, it certainly would have been oxtail soup!

The dear women, never having seen an American woman, just had to linger and look at this one with white skin and blue eyes. One of them said, "She is just as pretty as an eggshell! What made her white?" Perhaps that was the time when someone said, "I know. She drinks cow's milk!"

It was eleven o'clock by the time they had all looked enough and left, and we were in bed. I was just too tired to follow my good habit of being asleep in two minutes. Too, I soon found more living creatures than just the ox in that room. What my fellow missionary Dr. Jeannette Beall calls "China's millions," were crawling from the bed below, all over me, biting as they crawled. What could I do about that number-one enemy of China's poor?

For a moment I was tempted to be upset; then I prayed, "Lord, I am not here on a pleasure trip; I am here to tell these people about you. I cannot see them tomorrow unless I rest. Down in Egypt you sent the very small animals scampering at your rebuke. Now just turn the heads of these lice in another direction and let me sleep." In a moment I was fast asleep and never saw another one in my bedding.

Never did people or ox receive such attention! At the break of dawn the feeding began. First a daughter-in-law came with a basket of finely cut wheat straw, a bowl of wheat bran, and a pan of water, and stirred with a stick which rubbed against the stone trough. When she had gone, another came to stir, and called to the former to bring what was lacking in the proper proportion, the real motive of her visit being to look at the American while she slept.

The first morning I forgave all, knowing that farmers like to get an early start to work. But when the lazy old ox stood leisurely chewing his cud all day long, I asked if he could not be fed a little later. The lady of the house replied, "An ox must be fed at the same time every day if he keeps fat!" Only a day or two was he led out to plow.

With crowds following us everywhere we went, it was difficult to get a place to pray. Mrs. Han and I would put the women and children out of the room and close the crippled door, appointing someone to stand guard. We could then claim the promise of the two agreed, and pray for the Holy Spirit to use the Word we were giving, to work in the people's hearts.

That prayer time, however, did not take the place of my being alone with the Lord, where I could talk to him out loud and depend upon the promise to the one calling upon him in the secret place. Trying the shade of a big tree out in the field, I was surprised to be let alone. Upon returning, I found women distressed over my having ventured to a tree that "had a god in it." While pained over their superstition, I rejoiced to learn that one quiet spot was mine. Before the week was over, the Lord sent along a farmer and some little boys, who, from hearing the gospel, had lost all fear except the consequences of their own sin.

During the day Mrs. Han and I went from one courtyard to another. Usually the women were sitting on straw mats, taking apart quilts and winter clothes for washing. Where sheets are not used, this task must be done once a year. Each member of the family has his own quilt which he folds as an envelope and slides into from one end. He then takes off his wadded clothes and carefully spreads them on top of the quilt.

The poor people must take their winter clothes apart, not only for washing, but also because the top and lining are used separately and two summer garments are made from one winter one. Before cold weather the cotton will be cleaned and fluffed up and put in again. Alas, winter always catches some families before they get all the winter garments put back together.

Sitting on the mats beside the women, we explained to them their sinful state, their failure to glorify God and worship him, and what the loving Lord had done about their sins. We told them that God's Son, also being God, had taken their sins upon himself and taken their punishment.

Some replied to us, "I can't read; I am just a pan of starch, too stupid to understand anything new."

They could understand other things. We were amazed at their ability in running the home. The women would buy the exact amount of cloth for each child's new garment—so many feet and inches—and not half an inch would be left after the cutting. They also had sense for the most intricate gambling games.

In the evenings the group met on a big threshing floor. My kerosene lantern was hung on the mud wall, and my Bible verses, written on strips of paper with pictures and posters to illustrate them, were held in place by thorns from nearby bushes. One hour of sitting on the ground and listening was such a good start that all wanted two.

The men worked in the fields as long as they could see, and the supper had to be cooked after they got home, lest an extra wheat root would have to be burnt to keep it hot. So it was

nine o'clock before we could begin our service. This late beginning, of course, made bedtime very late.

One day Mrs. Han asked our hostess if she could keep the
family a little quiet in the early mornings so the missionary
could get the sleep she needed. The next morning our hostess
woke me up to tell me that she would keep the daughters-in-
law and children quiet, "So you just go right on sleeping," she
said.

The vegetable and millet market came to a village every
fifth day. When it came our turn, it was Sunday and we would
not buy. The next market day was in a village too far away, so
we found ourselves with no food. We could buy eggs in the
village, but no hens. Hens were laying, and no Chinese woman
would make such a poor business deal as to sell a laying hen.
We had to buy a rooster, which we could not boil tender. Mrs.
Han, the Bible woman, put a piece of saltpeter in the pot, and
the rooster got tender; but she got to eat him—I couldn't.

When we began to cook and eat, the flies always arrived.
When it rained more and more of them came. What better
shelter for a fly than an ox stall! Big ones and little ones, black
ones and green ones flew in! Not being able to sit under my
tree, the only way I could get alone was to walk the little
paths through the fields in the mud, where I could cry to the
Lord, the God of Israel.

I said, "I am one of your spoiled children. All my life I have
been accustomed to screened houses and clean food. Now, I
just can't eat with those flies all over my food. Down in Egypt
you had flies come and go at your word. You are the same today and you are ready to work in the same way if my situation
demands it. Now please do one of two things for me: either
take the flies away, or enable me just to go ahead and eat and
not mind them. You then take care of any disease germs which
they may put into my body. Just whichever you wish to do will
be good enough for me!"

Certainly he would grant one of the two requests. I was his
child and there in obedience to his command to tell people

about him. Which do you think he did? Not a fly flew into that
ox stall the remaining five days that I was there witnessing and
teaching!

You will agree that was a miracle. I can tell you one bigger
than that!

When we came to the last night of the meeting, it had rained
so no one could sit on the ground. Kaffir corn stalks were
brought and put on the side for the women to sit on, but the
children and the men just squatted in front of me. The children, after their choruses, memory verses, and Bible story,
soon tired of their squatting position and scampered off home
to bed, leaving a vacant space between me and the group of
men.

Feeling that some with whom Mrs. Han and I had no opportunity for personal talks might be ready to come to the Saviour, I invited such to come forward. I would have been
thrilled had one come. To my joy, the whole group of men just
came squatting up.

We missionaries did not teach the Chinese to pray. We just
told them that anyone could approach the holy God if he came
to him through his Son, the only mediator. I urged those men to
open their mouths as well as their hearts, in confession of sin
and in thanksgiving for Christ's death for them.

What a volume of prayer in that undertone! I could only
distinguish the words of the one at my feet as he thanked the
Lord for taking the punishment for his wine drinking, opium
smoking, gambling, and bad disposition. Eight or ten had
previously come to our room one by one and knelt at the foot
of the cross in humble confession and faith and gone away rejoicing.

If those people were born of the Spirit, that was the greatest
miracle of all earth's wonders. "Cooties" and flies have no en-
mity against God in their nature; but when a human being
realizes that he is deserving of hell, admits his guilt, and will-
ingly turns away from sin and chooses Christ as his Lord, that
is a miracle!

Journeying Mercies

Thanks be unto God, which always causeth us to triumph in Christ.
2 Corinthians 2:14

I had not been in Tsining many months when, on account of
Mrs. Connely's illness, Dr. Connely asked me to take an engagement for him. It was at a Bible conference for Chinese
preachers and Bible women of the Pochow and Kweiteh fields
of Anhui Province. Knowing only twenty-four hours before
starting that I was to go, I was tempted to tremble over the
thought of giving two messages a day to the Christian workers, including missionaries. However, I had learned that one
cannot tremble and trust at the same time, and I dared not go
without trusting.

I had remarked to Mr. Tai, the young preacher who was to
be the other speaker, that perhaps my dread in going to the
meeting was due to the fear that my Chinese language would
not be as good as that of the older missionaries who would be
present. He exclaimed, "Mercy on us! May the Lord save us
from going over there with the sin of pride in our hearts!" We
went down on our knees to get rid of it.

At the first railway junction we went to a little inn to await
the next train. We were on our knees praying for the conference when the "bellboy" appeared in the open door and asked,
"Are you ready for cigarettes?" Seeing that we were not quite
ready, he left us alone!

After five hours' travel to Hsuchow railway center, just over
the border of Kiangsu Province, and as many hours west into
Honan Province, we were at the city of Kweiteh. The remaining forty miles were covered in the mission's Model T Ford.
Upon arrival, we had touched four provinces, been enroute
thirty hours (not counting the Sunday spent at Kweiteh), and
spent only $2.50 each in U. S. money! We had traveled third-
class, there being no fourth, and had saved three-fourths of
the first-class fare! On two of the trains our coaches were like
freight boxcars with long benches running along the sides.

A big snow fell the first day of the conference, and the coldest wind of the winter blew in at every door and window of the unheated church building. Like Nehemiah, those in attendance were doing a great work and could not be disturbed, not even by the weather. Of course it took more time to get ready for the day, when all the winter clothing had to be put on. But I had learned that enough of the right kind of clothes would keep one comfortable in the coldest weather—well, warm, if not comfortable, for the burden of the clothes prevents the use of that word "comfortable."

The Lord was with us during the meeting—hearing all our prayers and using the Word that was being proclaimed—so nothing else mattered. Some were saved during the time. Others were revived and brought their besetting sins and weights to the foot of the cross. A number of the Chinese co-workers seemed to get a new vision of their opportunity to serve the Lord. When the ten days were over, our hearts were overflowing with praise to God.

Although our getting back to the railway over the forty miles of snow-covered road had been committed to the Heavenly Father, the Model T refused to run. And no owner of mules would send his precious animals out on a two-day-and-return trip to Kweiteh over such roads. The only other possibility for transportation was what people called "the bus." The agent claimed that by leaving at five in the morning, the trip could be made while the ground was still frozen. Warmer weather during the middle of the day would turn the road to mud.

Even though we had not been able to retire early the night before, we were up at three o'clock the morning we were to leave and at the station on time, with tickets in hand. When the bus, a five-passenger car, rolled out, seven men—fat from their winter "quilts" (clothes)—scrambled into it with their arms full of bundles. The outside of the car was piled high with their bedding rolls, bicycles, baskets, and suitcases. The agent kept telling us to get in if we wanted to go!

Eight passengers were left standing. That many would justify the cost of sending another car. But gasoline had been provided for only one car, and more gas could be secured only inside the city after the gates would open at six o'clock.

About seven o'clock, ten gallons of gas were finally obtained and put into a small truck the size of a Jeep. The truck had no springs, no self-starter, and no disposition to be cranked. After a time of pushing, the engine started. There being no step, I climbed in at the back, as gracefully as my heavy costume permitted.

Two little wooden benches about six inches wide, and too high for any Chinese, ran lengthwise in the truck bed. They were not stationary until we all were packed on them. But only three or four hours, I thought, and the forty miles would be ended. Humpty-dump we went over the frozen ridges, thinking that we would be shaken into nerves and aches and pains of all sorts.

Oh, if that bumpy traveling could have lasted! The snow on the road began to melt into a slush which made pulling so difficult the engine boiled every few minutes. A "footman" with a five-gallon tin of water hung on to a fender. When the driver didn't have to stop to let the engine cool, he had to stop at a well for the footman to refill the tin. Usually with the halting, the engine went "dead" and all had to climb out and push!

Then a tire went flat! We had to wait an hour in the mud and slush, which got deeper all the time. The passengers who wanted to get home for the Chinese New Year reviled the driver and complained in true human fashion. Mr. Tai and I were able, by the Lord's abundant grace, to keep a patient, Christian spirit. And, gradually, we saw a change in the attitude of others.

Mr. Tai loaned his gloves to the driver and was the first one to help push and the last to give up. I pushed once, but seeing the engine unable to appreciate my assistance, I just saved my energy to endure the ride.

That day we went twenty miles and used seven and one-half gallons of the gas. In the evening, we stopped at an inn. As the passengers and the footman sat around in the courtyard, they heard why and how they must be born again. A high official who had sat by the driver and who had not been able to help push the truck because of the weight of the silver dollars in his military belt was inside smoking his opium.

Two Mohammedan women seemed to be hearing of the Saviour for the first time. Their roll of bedding, which had been tied on the outside of the car, was wet and muddy. But I bought a bowl of fire-coals and dried two quilts a bit, one for Mr. Tai and the other for the women and myself. The board-bed was too narrow for three people, but another wide board like the two original ones was laid on two stools beside them, and the bed was complete! With my fur coat spread over me, I slept warmer than I did "soft"!

The poor footman had to sit up for lack of bedding, so the night seemed long to him. He called us at midnight, at 2:00 A.M., and again at 4:00, asking us to get up. He wanted to tie on the baggage so it would be ready by the driver's starting time.

However, we need not have rushed, for the kerosene added to the gas did not improve the starting ability of the engine. It was eight o'clock before our souls were delighted with the engine's first "hiss."

We were flying along, making nearly fifteen miles an hour, when the young officer who was packed in just back of the driver's seat suddenly exclaimed, "My nose must be blown!" Now that *was* a problem, for a handkerchief is no part of a Chinese soldier's equipment. The only opening of the bus was at the rear. He reached it by stretching himself full length over the crowded knees of all, while we had a refreshing laugh.

The next excitement was another flat tire, and all of us jumped out. I had become a near-athlete by that time.

The silver-dollar-burdened official marched up and down the roadside to keep warm. I saw in the old tire-burst an opportunity to speak to this official. While not knowing what to say, I trusted the Lord to put the right words into my mouth. Politely greeting him, I said, "You do not have to be bound by sin! The Lord Jesus Christ can set you free," and walked away.

The official called Mr. Tai to know what I had meant, and after a few minutes Mr. Tai went away, leaving the man with something to think about. Soon he called Mr. Tai again, and after the two had gone aside for thirty minutes, the official came to tell me that he had become a Christian. He confessed to being burdened with more weights than silver, and bound by more sins than opium.

A family nearby were kind enough to warm us by burning some of their grass fuel on the floor (ground) of their reception room. That visit gave me an opportunity to tell them about my Saviour. The donkey tied at one side went on with his breakfast, undisturbed by the smoke and ashes, or by the message of sin and the Saviour.

When the truck finally was pushed off by the villagers, Mr. Tai and I praised God for the stop, even though during the delay the ground had thawed and the mud-sticking had begun. The car proved more difficult to start than the day before. However, having committed that day's travel to the Lord, who calls things that are not as though they were (Rom. 4:7), I did not fear an explosion of the kerosene in the engine.

Finally we reached the station. We had time before the train arrived to go to an inn and buy some food and to get the first layer of mud brushed off. At the inn we met a Christian army officer and his wife who were away from home, church, and all Christian acquaintances. While they were keeping up their family worship, they said, it had "no flavor" because they were living defeated lives. Mr. Tai was able to encourage them and give spiritual food.

The cold train traveled with the speed and smoothness of a freight, and the hard benches were too high. But what a relief not to have to get out and push! About midnight we were at Hsuchow again, where we were to catch a north-bound train for home at 7:00 A.M. Mr. Tai didn't think it worth the money to go to an inn, but, to me, the shorter the time the more precious the rest. We chose the best inn advertised, thirty cents a room with iron beds and springs. But, alas, the beds had no mattress, and quilts were ten cents apiece extra! However, those beds brought "beauty rest," compared with the beds of the night before.

The next evening at six o'clock we reached our homes, too tired to hold up our heads any longer. But we were grateful, beyond words to express, for all the ways in which the dear Lord had smiled upon us.

My Ears

What is man, that thou art mindful of him? Psalm 8:4

In 1933 I began having a buzz in one of my ears. The ear specialist of Peking Union Medical College Hospital diagnosed the trouble as the eardrums becoming concave. He told me that I would gradually lose my hearing, for no medical science could prevent a convex eardrum from becoming concave. I *thought* that I turned the matter over to the Lord immediately. I returned home and told the Connelys that when I could no longer hear, I would not annoy my friends pretending that I could, but would admit deafness and use a hearing aid.

When I told a visitor from America about the diagnosis, she replied, "If I were you, I would not accept deafness like that! If I were a missionary called to do the work that you are, I would take my ears to the Lord and ask him to heal them now!" After that, I began daily adding to my prayers, "Lord, heal my ears if it be thy will." However, nothing was made definite, and no doubt I would have been surprised had my ears been healed.

Two years later I was working alone in Tsining. Our church had no pastor and I had heard no preaching for more than a year, except my own and that which a few laymen could do, which was even poorer than mine! I became hungry to hear good preaching. Our church invited Pastor Fan Wei Ming, pastor of the big city church over in Hwanghsien and vice president of our North China seminary, to come and preach for a week.

When he arrived, my ears were buzzing, first one and then the other. This was most annoying, and I imagined that I was not hearing well.

Knowing that Pastor Fan had been used in praying for the sick, I asked him the first day to pray for my ears to be healed. He put me off in an indefinite manner and went on majoring on his main theme, "Christians should live holy lives." Using the feasts of the Old Testament, he reminded us that the Feast of Unleavened Bread, when all leaven must be put out, preceded the Feast of Pentecost. He urged us to search the heart for any leaven, which he made typical of sin.

Wanting to co-operate in the meetings and be blessed, I began praying for the Lord to show me the leaven in my heart and life. He showed me a few things. One of these was the fact that I had formerly considered that one-tenth of my possessions was the Lord's and the nine-tenths my own to use as I liked. I was convinced that in the future I must seek the Lord's will in advance for the way every cent of the nine-tenths should be spent.

Twice daily we went to church, and each time the power of the Lord was upon the speaker. He showed us from the Word how holy we must live in order to have fellowship with the Lord and see his power flow through us to others.

One day at the table I burst out crying and exclaimed, "I have said that if the Lord willed for me to be deaf, I was willing, but I did not know what I was saying! I do not have to hear conversation that belongs to this world, but if I cannot go to the house of God and hear his Word preached, I cannot live! I just cannot be deaf!"

Pastor Fan only admonished me to turn my ears over to the Lord. At the church, he went on with the kind of preaching that kept us searching our hearts. After a few more days, I was made to realize something of the exceeding sinfulness of my own heart. "Take out leaven? I am nothing *but* leaven! I can-

not take out my very self! The poison of the devil is in my nature!" What a black sight! I could neither eat nor sleep and
tears streamed down. Just the thought of what I was by nature
gave me the physical backache.

At three services I was the first to respond to the altar call.
No marvel that the King of glory had to come down to this
sinful world and take a human body. Someone had to take the
punishment for all that I was, which was unlike holy God, and
only God in the flesh could do that. How I had used my ears
to sin! All my life I had reveled in compliments. The pride of
life! Those ears were presented to the Lord for his cleansing,
like Isaiah's lips of old, which only could be cleansed by coals
from off the altar.

The last Sunday afternoon of the meeting a few gathered in
my living room, so heart-hungry that they could not let the
meetings come to a close without a new uplift from the Lord.
Heaven opened and God began to pour joy into our souls. I
could only kneel by the chair and laugh, as one wave of joy
after another came. Those who could put their praise into
words prayed, but I just let them speak for me. Later Pastor
Fan asked me if I still wanted prayer for my ears. A number of
Scripture passages were suggested, among them Exodus 4:11,
"Who maketh the dumb, or deaf . . . ? Have not I the Lord?"

While I was reading the various passages, there was a
physical sensation on each side of my face as if tight tendons
were loosening up. Pastor Fan then read from James 5 and
prayed.

I had previously felt keenly the burden of the work in the
five counties. But absolute relaxation now came. I did not
have a responsibility in the world! All that I had to do was
just to stand there and let the Lord do what he wanted to do
through me.

But while I was so joyous in my soul, my ears were still
buzzing, and after a few days, they began to ache. They had
never hurt before that time. Now, one would buzz and the
other ache, then both would buzz and both ache. Thinking

that it was the devil trying to make me doubt that the ears were healed, I held on to the Lord's will for my ears and endured the discomfort.

After about a month, when the pain was almost unbearable, I said, "Lord, you know that these ears are not mine! They were definitely given over to you, and since they are yours, they cannot hurt unless you let them hurt. Now if you do, it will be for some purpose and you will enable me to stand it, I know."

After another week or two the pain and buzzing completely stopped.

Two years later, after having gone through the Japanese War alone, I came on furlough. While it is the Board's policy for furloughing missionaries to go for a checkup, the Board's secretary, supposing that I was a nervous wreck, suggested I go immediately to my state Baptist hospital, stay as long as necessary, and get all the treatment needed.

When the ear specialist had completed his examination, I asked, "Are my eardrums growing in?"

"Why did you ever think that?" he replied.

When I told him what the ear specialist of the hospital in Peking had said a few years before, he said, "I cannot understand such a diagnosis! Your eardrums are in perfect condition!"

I then added, "Something happened after that. We prayed for them to be healed, and if they are all right now, it is because the Lord worked in them."

"Faith can do great things, if you have it!" he quietly answered me.

To me, it was not our faith, but just the loving Lord making it possible for me to continue to go to the house of God and hear his Word preached! When the doctor had pronounced my ear drums in perfect condition, I realized that the buzzing and aching which followed the prayer for healing had been caused by the necessary physical readjustment of the drums.

The Lily of the Valley

I am made all things to all men, that I might by all means save some.
1 Corinthians 9:22

Soon after being transferred to Tsining in 1933, I met Mr. Huang, the city councilman for our section, called in Chinese "the street elder." He came several times a year to collect the quarterly taxes, or to inform us of some new regulation which the city council had passed, such as every household co-operating with the fire department by keeping a barrel of water by the front gate.

I always took advantage of the contacts with Mr. Huang to tell him something about the Saviour. Being of the old school and too polite to look at a woman, he would sit with his eyes on the corner of the room and completely exasperate me by saying, "All religions are good! Buddhism is good; Taoism is good; Confucianism is good; Mohammedanism is good; and Christianity is also good!" My Lord and Saviour was not even to be mentioned the same day with these man-made religions!

A few years later Mr. Huang came sauntering through my yard, dressed in a rich tan satin brocade toga that just cleared the ground. He had an air of possessing the universe.

A Presbyterian friend leaving on furlough had sent some of his tulip bulbs to me. Never were flowers watched with more eagerness or enjoyed with more delight than those red, yellow, and purple blooms. When the Christians admired them, I told them that when they multiplied, I would share them.

Seeing my tulips, Mr. Huang began to exclaim and ask all about them. Of course I could not tell the proud Mr. Huang that I would give him some bulbs when they had multiplied. But when he had gone, I put three of the prettiest tulips in a pot and sent them over to his home with my card.

Another time I had a lily of the valley in my garden. The sprigs had been given to Mary Connely, who entrusted the plant to me when she left for the States. I watched over it with the same tender care she had. Imagine my joy when the early days of May brought up those first three dainty, fragrant blooms.

The next day, over came Mr. Huang, profusely repeating his thanks for the tulips and strutting through the yard in peacock fashion to see what else had bloomed. Lo! he spied the lily of the valley! He even humbled himself enough to smell it, and asked many questions about it.

When he had gone, I said, "I am after Mr. Huang's soul, and if it is going to take Mary Connely's lily of the valley to win him, it will have to go!" I put the blooming portion in a pretty little pot and sent it over.

Mr. Huang came over immediately, exuberant in his thanks, and acting so much like an old friend that I invited him in. He sat and looked at me while I told him of the mighty God having become flesh in order to die, and doing so in order to take the punishment for my sins and his. After listening attentively, he went home with a copy of one of the Gospels and some tracts.

The following Sunday evening Mr. Huang was sitting on the back seat at church, looking amazed at himself for being there. The next Sunday he was a few benches down the aisle, and by the third Sunday he was halfway to the front of the church.

By the end of the summer Mr. Huang had gotten to the second bench from the front. In the meantime, he had been to my home many times, each time hearing more about the Lord and taking home more and more gospel tracts.

Since our church had no pastor or preacher at that time, I had to lead many of the church services. One Sunday evening in September Mr. Huang sat drinking in the message of Amos 4:12, "Prepare to meet thy God." At the close, I asked anyone who wanted to get ready to meet God to get on his knees where he was. I expected so many that there would not be room for them at the front. Imagine my joy at seeing that proud man go down on his knees before the Lord!

The next week, Mr. Huang started attending the early

morning Bible class and prayer meeting at six o'clock. After
a few months of daily searching the Scriptures, he was sure
enough of his salvation to make a public confession and ask
for baptism. He sent his children to the mission school and
one by one they turned to the Lord. The two oldest, a son
and a daughter who were in high school, volunteered for
Christian work. His wife and other near relatives were saved.
Hurrah for the lily of the valley!

Tyranny

*The wicked plotteth against the just, and gnasheth upon him with his
teeth. Psalm 37:12*

The happy Christian Huang family prayed and longed for
deliverance from the Japanese, little dreaming that a greater
enemy would soon arise from within their own land. Their
treatment when the Communists occupied their city is an illustration of the tyranny of the so-called People's Government
of China.

Mr. Huang had supported his family for years on rent from
a number of residences which he owned in the city of Tsining.
When the Japanese took the city, they commandeered the
houses and used them during the eight years in which they
occupied East China.

Upon the withdrawal of the Japanese, Mr. Huang resumed
control of his houses and again rented them.

When the Communists came, needing living quarters, they
accused Mr. Huang of having taken property which did not
belong to him. Officials put the occupants out and moved into
the residences themselves.

Because Mr. Huang protested, his wife was arrested and
kept in prison for several weeks. She was then tried by the
new court of the city, which was composed of street urchins
and "down-and-outers."

Mrs. Huang was still in prison during the trial and was not
permitted to have a lawyer or anyone to speak in her behalf.

A Communist official who was presiding at "court" asked of

what the woman was accused. A little boy arose and stated that, during the previous summer, in the rainy season when he was wading in the street in front of the Huang home, Mrs. Huang came out and slapped him on the face. Two other urchins made accusations which were just as absurd.

The official went into a rage and asked what punishment the People's court would suggest for such a terrible woman.

One of the little boys who had accused her, having forgotten what he had been primed to say, arose and shouted, "I move that we fine her five thousand dollars!" At this, the chairman yelled out, "You mean *fifty* thousand dollars!" The boy assented, "Yes! Yes! Fifty thousand dollars!"

The city officials then confiscated everything that the Huangs possessed, even their clothes, and sold all, leaving the family paupers.

6

The
Japanese
Come

In 1934 Martha Franks was transferred to Hwanghsien to work in our North China Baptist Seminary. In the spring of 1936 the Connelys went to America on furlough, where for health reasons they were kept for two and a half years. I was the only Baptist missionary left at Tsining.

The Lord's Guidance

In all thy ways acknowledge him, and he shall direct thy paths. Proverbs 3:6

The latter part of July, 1937, I went up to Taishan, fifty miles away, for a few weeks' rest. While there a call came from the United States Consulate asking me to proceed to the coast. However, on the morning of August 1 there was an earthquake that made even the greatest mountain in East China, Taishan, jerk and quiver. Since no small damage was done in Tsining, it was necessary for me to return there to see about property repairs.

Upon reaching Tsining, I found a city alarmed indeed. Before plans for repairs of our property were completed, more urgent calls came from the Consulate advising me to proceed to the coast at once before railway lines were broken, making escape impossible.

With no pastor at the Tsining city church, how could I leave the sheep without a shepherd, at such a time! I was burdened also for inexperienced Chinese co-workers in surrounding counties on the Tsining field who would have no one to consult about the work. However, there seemed no alternative except to go, so I packed to be gone indefinitely.

The Christians gathered in the yard while I stood on the steps of the Connely residence and read to them the Forty-sixth Psalm. The more mature understood that I was leaving in order to co-operate with my Government. To others, it meant that I was pointing them to the Lord for protection, while going to a safer place myself.

On the way to port I met one freight train after another with loads of people inside, between the coaches, and on top of the boxcars, all fleeing to the interior. And upon arrival in Tsingtau I found a city that seemed to be dying fast. Most shops were closed, and foodstuffs were soaring in prices.

No sooner had Alda Grayson, Mary Crawford, and I rented rooms, set up housekeeping, and made out a program of work in Tsingtau, when the consulate advised us to leave for the United States. The daily paper announced that President Roosevelt urged all Americans, without exception, to leave China. The Government would not be responsible for protection of any who chose to remain.

How would we answer? The President had not sent us to China. Twelve years previously I had asked our Foreign Mission Board secretary to accept a statement from me requesting that nothing should be said if I should lose my life or any amount of earthly goods in China. The Lord had carried me to China. During the coming months and years, China would need missionaries as never before.

Those who chose to remain had to accept the fact that one place was about as safe as another, except, of course, the actual battle front. Of the nearly one thousand people who already had been killed by one bomb explosion in Shanghai, nearly all had been Chinese who had fled there for safety.

Hospital workers were not only *permitted*, but *expected* to remain at their posts, and I was reminded that in "Christian wars," chaplains also are permitted to remain in war zones. While chaplains are men, women on the mission field often have to do the work which men do not go to do.

For two and a half months I remained in Tsingtau, where

I had a good vacation and helped with the mission work. One day, I knew in my heart that the Lord wanted me to return to Tsining and stand by those people in their suffering. I went to the American Consulate and reported that I was returning, as I always wanted the Government to know exactly where I would be.

Trains were running only at night to avoid being bombed. The eleven hours' travel from Tsingtau to the capital of the province, Tsinan, was a long night of joyful praise to the Lord for the privilege of returning to the Chinese Christians, to stand with them in their dark hour and take what they would have to take.

After spending a day in Tsinan, I took another train that night. It may have been well that I could not see the bombed trains along the way.

What had been fear in the hearts of people before I went away, had become panic, as men and women rushed from one place to another to find shelter. Women were actually losing their minds, and children were screaming in their helplessness.

Never did one receive such a welcome! The Christians said to me, "Since you are not afraid and can trust the Lord and come back, we will trust him and quit being afraid."

We opened our church for service every evening. People who had not formerly been interested in the gospel came. The city was filled with refugees from northern cities which had already fallen to the Japanese, and many of them came. Sometimes the church could not hold the crowd and some had to go away.

Two teachers were able to take turns with me in leading services. We always gave an opportunity for any who wanted to be saved to come forward and wait for an after-meeting. Knowing that many of the people soon would be moving on west to keep ahead of the incoming army, I wanted to get those who were being saved clearly established in the Lord before they left. One evening I suggested that any wanting personal help come to my house at the noon hour. To my surprise, thirty-five came. I put them into a class which met daily at the church.

We were having, as usual, our early morning Bible class and prayer meeting which had been going for ten years.

So many wounded were being sent back from the front that the one hospital was soon filled; the high school was closed to make room; large private homes were commandeered; and some stores were ordered to pack up their goods and turn their buildings into places for the wounded. I gave my afternoons to the hospital, where I had been especially invited. It was two miles away, but I never took a ricksha because I would have passed hundreds of people who were there that day but might be dead the next. Walking both ways, I could hand out a gospel tract to everyone I passed.

Thus I lived for eight busy weeks, trying to make every moment count for eternity. Most of the morning time was spent seeing callers who came for various reasons, then preparing for Bible classes and evening meetings. But I did guard the time for my own prayer and devotional Bible study. I knew that no matter how busy I might be for the Lord, I would soon become useless unless I took time for my personal fellowship with him day by day.

One Saturday after I had gone at that speed for a month, a man who had attended some of the night meetings waited after the noon class, saying that he wanted to be saved. We got on our knees before the open Bible and started reading verse after verse on sin and its consequences, comparing man with God's holy standard for him.

Just to be sure that he knew what sin was, I asked, "Mr. Wang, what is the greatest sin you ever committed?" To my astonishment, he replied, "Murder." In a family feud he had killed a man, and because all in the village were related, the murderer was protected.

What a glorious message I had for a murderer! I showed him that while, according to God's holy law, he deserved to forfeit his own life for such a sin, the Lord Jesus Christ had done just that in his stead. It took two hours to lead that man to where he was rejoicing in the Saviour. What a change came over his face!

That one trophy would have been sufficient reward for all that I endured during the war, had I been looking for rewards. Day after day the expression on the man's face changed, as peace and joy took the place of fear and distress. At that time the Chinese Government of the city had gone west. It was not necessary for him to confess and surrender to a Japanese government when they assumed control.

When I reached home after that "new birth," it was three o'clock, too late to go to the hospital. I dropped on my knees and asked the Lord what to do with these two hours before supper and the evening meeting. Immediately, I thought of a young couple who, some months before, had shown interest in the Lord. I had not heard of them since returning to the city. I supposed that the Lord wanted me to visit them. But that was not according to reason! They lived as far away as was the hospital.

I began to feel myself to see if I were not too tired. For the last month I had not sat down even five minutes a day to rest. And anyway, who from South Carolina would not want Saturday afternoon off!

Some weeks before, I had put L. L. Legter's little book on the fulness of the Holy Spirit on the arm of my comfortable chair to read, but, not having sat in the chair, I had not opened it. With myself I reasoned, "I just know that it would please the Lord for me to sit down and relax and read this little book." But the few paragraphs which I read had no "flavor," and my heart was uncomfortable.

Taking my tract-bag, I started; but on reaching the end of the first block, where I should have turned north, I felt drawn to go south. Without arguing with the Lord, I just turned south. In the middle of the block I met a man in civil service uniform, to whom I handed a tract. He was surprised indeed at seeing an American woman in that part of China at such a time. I told him of the evening meetings at the church around the corner and invited him to come.

Reaching the next corner, I felt no leading to continue south, so I turned north and went on and outside the east city gate to make the call. Returning, walking faster than anyone on the street, I handed everyone a tract and invited each to the evening meetings.

As I passed another man in the same kind of civil service uniform, he said as he took the leaflet, "I approve of this! My wife's people in Tsiensin are Christians." When I reached the church, the first man whom I had met on the street was on the front seat, and a little later the second man came. They waited for the after-meeting and in a few days both were clearly saved.

The Lord's Reward

The Lord directeth his steps. Proverbs 16:9

On my visits to the hospital I was never able to get around even one time to all the men in one ward. And every day some died without hearing of the Saviour.

One day when I stopped outside the big ward on the second floor where I, humanly speaking, should have gone, I asked the Lord where to spend the next three hours. I felt led to go to the third-floor ward. Without debating that I had been there the day before, I went.

By the side of a bed was a fifteen-year-old soldier boy who had come to visit his wounded friend. Upon finding that the boy knew nothing whatever of the gospel, I invited him to attend the night meeting at our church. When he told me that his company was just passing through the city and would be there only one night, I suggested that he attend the one night. City gates were closed at dark and he did not know whether his company would be billeted outside or inside the city walls, but, if inside, he promised to attend. I told him there what I could about the Lord in the few minutes that I could give to one person, being aided by the patient who had heard a little the day before.

At the evening service I looked everywhere for the lad but did not see him. However, he had been lost in the crowd and, at the close of the service, came forward wanting to be saved. He was led to the Lord by a young teacher who left him rejoicing with a New Testament. After a few weeks I received a letter from the boy, written from a western province. He thanked us for having led him to the living Lord and added that if he had to give his life for his country, he would not be afraid, since he knew that he would go to his Saviour.

One Sunday night at church I noticed on the back seat a fine-looking young man in an army aviator's uniform. The next evening he was a few benches forward, and the third evening he was near enough to the front for me to reach him with tracts before he got out. The fifth night, he came forward and remained for the after-meeting. I suggested that he come to my house the next afternoon so that some of the young men in the church could help him.

He arrived at 2:00 P.M. Mr. Tai, a local young man who had finished at our North China seminary and had been preaching in the eastern part of the province, had just come home to preach in Tsining. He was a good personal worker as well as a splendid preacher. He was there to help me. With Bible and posters we began teaching. The aviator was especially impressed by a poster portraying the broad and narrow ways. The gate to the narrow way represented Christ, and the way was only wide enough for the person himself to enter without his bundle of sin.

While we were talking, praying, and yearning for the aviator to have the truth revealed to his heart by the Holy Spirit, Mr. Ma and Mr. Yen arrived. In July, Ma Ying Tang, superintendent of education for the county, had been saved. Afterwards, he brought his friend, Mr. Yen, with him to church. As was my custom when a new face appeared at church, I had set my prayers upon him.

Upon returning from Tsingtau, I had learned that Mr. Yen was an official in a county seat a few hours by train to the south of Tsining. I wrote him a letter urging him to turn to the Lord. He said that he had been interested in becoming a Christian since Mr. Ma was saved. Upon receiving my letter, he became so eager that he got excused from the office for the day to come to Tsining!

What an opportunity! We read and explained and illustrated, trying to enable both Mr. Yen and the aviator to see that God had already done his best when Jesus became his Lamb to die, that their sinful selves and all of their sins might be put on him. After a while, seeing that they understood with their minds, I stated that it was now a matter of their wills. They must choose to make Christ Lord, as he would not come into their hearts otherwise.

When I asked for their decision, Mr. Teng, the aviator, replied, "I want to enter the narrow gate." Mr. Yen expressed the same desire, so we got on our knees before the Lord. Mr. Tai prayed, I prayed, and then Mr. Ma prayed most fervently for them.

I asked if either Mr. Yen or the aviator had anything they wanted to say to the Lord. Mr. Yen began pouring out his heart in confession of sin, then of faith in Christ's death. When he had finished, Mr. Teng followed. By supper time they were rejoicing in release from sin and the indwelling presence of the Lord. What a glorious afternoon it had been!

Mr. Yen returned to his work and I never saw him again. But I rejoiced in the few letters written, as long as he could get them through.

Mr. Teng not only continued coming to the evening meetings but was able to arrange his daily schedule so he could attend our noon Bible class where he "devoured" the Word. An evening or two after his conversion, he brought another member of the air force, Mr. Chang, of whom he whispered on the side, "Prayer brought him." Within a few days Mr. Chang professed to be saved.

While Mr. Tai had been away in the eastern province, his wife suddenly lost her mind. Since I was the only one to whom she would listen, and that only occasionally, I had the responsibility of the crazy woman added to my other work. Instead of getting better when Mr. Tai arrived, as we had expected, she continually grew worse.

At midnight on the twenty-third of December, I was awakened by the sister of Mr. Tai calling that her sister-in-law had cut herself to death. Grabbing my fur garment, and some bed linen from the hall cabinet for bandages, I went running, in the hope that she had not died. But there lay that lovely young mother with her blood poured out. Her non-Christian mother was screaming in true heathen style, "Who will pity me! Who will pity me!"

Both children had been awakened. The three-year-old was crying because he knew what had taken place, and the younger because he did not know. The father and his high-school sister took the children over to my house, while I spent the rest of the night helping my servant prepare the body for burial.

Early the next morning we got a casket and had a little funeral service in the yard when the Christians came to the morning prayer service. We were able to get the burial over before the bombing planes came at nine o'clock.

The next night there was no sleep at my house, as the Tai baby, from change of food, cried all night.

Christmas

Let him take hold of my strength. Isaiah 27:5

Our mission yard was full of refugees. We took in the womenfolk of any male member of the church, whether or not the women themselves were Christians. They brought their flour or millet and little mud cookstoves and pots. At night their bedding rolls became pallets all over the place.

We had several basements to which they could go during

bombing raids, and each woman had her place assigned. The church basement was reserved for the men of the church during the actual siege of the city.

The victorious enemy drew nearer daily. As the cannon roar became louder and louder, our city people grew more panic-stricken. Daily more and more people left for the west. Shops were closed most of the day, and the bombers became more successful in their hits.

One afternoon when returning from my visit to the hospital, I found even the Christians in great excitement over the bomb that had been dropped just across the narrow street from our grounds. I kept quoting to them, "God is our refuge and strength. . . . Therefore will not we fear, though the earth be removed" (Psalm 46:1-2). It meant something when I stood with them and quoted it.

My own favorite was John 14:20: "I am in my Father, and ye in me, and I in you," said Jesus. How safe! Anything touching me would have to pass by God the Father, then it would have to get by Jesus Christ the Son, before it could reach me; and if it did, there would be the Lord inside of me, so filling me with himself that there would be no problem. What the Chinese friends called courage, boldness, strength, was Christ himself living his life in me. Now you may be sure that I had my sins forgiven up to date at such a time! I was not only keeping clean enough inside for him to dwell, but I was choosing his will in advance, daily and moment by moment.

Since Christ was faithful to the one who was trusting him, every day was filled with joy, with never a thought of what might happen, or of any personal danger. I was in the place to which the Lord had brought me, and if I should die with the others, it did not matter. I was completely possessed with the desire to do all that I could, for all the people that I could, while I could, *for the night would surely come!* What kind of night, no one knew!

As Christmas drew near, the church members wanted to follow their usual custom and have a meal together in the

church basement. But even the most well-to-do had no extra
money at a time like that, to help provide the dinner for those
who could not help themselves. Just when we had decided *not*
to have the dinner, twenty-five dollars arrived from the Connelys especially for that purpose. So, all was planned for noon
dinner on the twenty-fourth. It was thrilling to see the joy of
those who were having their first Christmas and to hear their
testimonies as to the change which had come to them.

While in Tsingtau the summer before, I got my first China
disease, amoebic dysentery. I entered the good hospital built
while the Germans were in control in that port, and within
ten days was released as well but advised to see a doctor
every two months for a checkup. Christmas Eve, just before
the two months were up, my old enemy, the amoebic dysentery came back!

It had been a miracle what the Lord enabled me as a well
woman to do at that time. Now I said, "Lord, I am the only
one you have to use here. With what is already on, and the
Japanese army only a few days from the city, I cannot afford
to be sick! In the name of my Lord and Saviour Jesus Christ,
I command this dysentery to leave me!" Not another symptom
of dysentery have I had since!

A group of Presbyterian missionaries lived in the south
suburb, two miles from the Baptist mission. They worked in
that section and in twenty counties, while the Baptists worked
inside the city and in five counties. We never overlapped. In
all my visits to the county seats and villages I saw only three
Presbyterians. Chinese are not disturbed by different denominations, as some people in America suppose. The Chinese are
accustomed to several divisions of Buddhism, which has prepared them for the work of different Christian denominations.

The missionaries of the two denominations in Tsining enjoyed precious fellowship in a little English worship service
held each week from home to home. Wedding anniversaries
and birthdays were celebrated with a "company dinner," when
each household provided part of the menu. On Christmas

Day we had a big time when a gift was provided for the one whose name we had drawn, while each had the privilege of taking something for the children. That year we had our dinner at noon on Christmas Day at a Presbyterian home, after which we sang carols in English to our heart's content.

Christmas night many came forward at the church service, wanting to know personally the Lord of whom they had been hearing. I had not been fazed thus far by my two nights' loss of sleep with the Tai baby. But that Christmas evening, I was so tired that I wondered if I could get upstairs to my room. However, I found Mr. Teng, the aviator, Mr. Wang, a teacher, and Mr. Ma, the superintendent of education, waiting to ask if I would pray with them through the night.

When I asked what they wanted to pray about, they answered, "For the church work, for our country, and for Mr. Tai." The latter was so crushed over not being able to keep his wife from suicide that he thought he could not preach again to others.

I told them that many Christians had the custom of spending the last night of the old year in prayer, thanking God for the past and seeking guidance for the incoming year. They stated that they might receive orders to go west before New Year's Day. I then suggested, "You do not need me to pray with you. You stay here where it is warm and pray as long as you like."

They replied, "We do not know where to find the Scripture passages which we will need. When you pray, you quote the promises of God. We cannot quote them from memory nor do we know where to find them in the Bible."

I asked that they give me just two nights to catch up on sleep, after which I would gladly pray with them. Two of them answered that they might have to leave the very next day. As I turned to go up to my room, I prayed, "Lord, shall I pray with them or shall I not?" The answer came back, "Could you not watch with me one hour?" I said, "Yes, Lord, through the strength which you will give, I can."

I began by telling them that there were some conditions for our praying together. The first was that no one but the four of us should know that we had prayed. I did not want to give the devil a chance to make them proud by having people speak of how warmhearted they were. The second condition was that we would not then decide to pray all night, as there was no virture in the amount of time one spent on his knees. We would pray until what was on our hearts had been put on the Lord and completely entrusted to him; then we would go to bed.

I read some Bible passages and soon we were on our knees before the Lord. I was just as refreshed as if it had been early morning after a good night's sleep.

Though all those men had sincerely trusted Christ as Saviour, they knew little of what that might mean in this life, until the Holy Spirit began to show them that Christ was Lord and King as well as Saviour. They began to see they must choose Christ's will in absolutely every detail of their lives and live for his glory only. This would entail their handing themselves over to him now. They would learn later that, even though all had been given over in a bundle, as it were, each new experience in life would require a new and definite committal of all that was involved.

One by one they struggled through, until each had put himself into the hands of the Lord to live for the extension of his kingdom. It was then 2:00 A.M., but no one had prayed for the church, for the country, or for the grief-stricken Mr. Tai. Knowing that they were then prepared to pray for others, I went to bed. When I went to sleep in the room above, they were still praying, but I never asked what time they reached their last "Amen."

Three days later, both Mr. Teng and Mr. Ma had to leave. Mr. Ma had to walk two hundred miles to West Honan. He left his baggage behind, but he carried his Bible and hymnbook and a copy of Jane Lide's book in Chinese on the New Testament church.

The Lord's Protection

The Lord shall be thy confidence. Proverbs 3:26

On the morning of January 10, 1937, a big silk store near us was bombed. The enemy army was only a day's march to the east. The morning of the 11th, I had callers with problems, making it about nine o'clock before I got away for my own quiet time with the Lord. While I was praying, I heard the buzzing of planes. Others on the place had heard the city signal announcing their coming and had gone to the basements and dugouts.

I had spiritual sense enough to know that the only way to be acceptable in God's holy presence was by identifying myself with Christ in his death. Because I was doing this I knew that the mighty Creator, the Sustainer of the Universe, was listening to me. I prayed, "Lord, there come those instruments of torture flying out of the pit of hell! [I did not mean from Japan—I meant from the devil himself!] Now, for the sake of these helpless people who have no way of escape, will you take charge of those planes! Hold the hands of the bombardiers and do not let those bombs fall anywhere on this city today except where you permit them to fall."

I knew that the Lord had heard me. Leaving the planes with him I went on praying for all who were attending the daily meetings. I called the names of those whom I knew and identified the others to the Lord, as the man with the gray scarf, the one with the red button on his black silk hat, the stooped one, or the student. One by one they were presented to the One who had power and love to reveal to their hearts the truth which they were hearing. I was so interested in getting everyone before the throne of grace, that I not only did not hear the planes again, but I even forgot about them.

About eleven o'clock I went down to my study for an hour's work with my Chinese secretary in preparation for the noon Bible class. He was writing in large Chinese characters the Bible verses which I wished to present to the group. We were both completely absorbed in what we were doing. The message from the Lord, I felt, must be just what the Lord wanted that day, for the next day we might not be living!

Suddenly our two-story brick house quivered, and window-panes were crushed out! I thought the bomb had struck the top of the house and supposed that all of the second story was knocked off. I was preserved in perfect calm. Not a sound from my lips! Not one irregular heartbeat! The very second that the bomb struck, I knew that God had permitted it for some purpose and it was all right.

I went to the basement of the residence where the people were screaming and yelling. When someone tried to show me the broken windows, I said, "The house does not matter now. I only came to see if anyone is hurt." Finding no one injured, I went out by the basement door to the yard.

The air was black from the gray brick and tiles that had been blown into powder. My little Chinese home was wrecked, the little pastorium down, other buildings damaged and our big trees cut.

In the little basement of the well tower stood Mr. Tai's mother with cuts on her face, holding one of the Tai babies in her arms. Seeing that none was seriously hurt, I started up the steps to the school. Mr. Tai, who was standing by his mother with the other crying baby in his arms, said, "Miss Smith, do not go out now."

I answered, "I am going to see if anyone is hurt."

He said again, "Please do not go out now!"

I replied, "A moment's delay might mean the loss of a life!" and started on up the steps.

"For Jesus' sake, I ask you not to go out now," he begged.

Stepping back down, I answered, "It was for Jesus' sake that I was going, but since you feel that way about it, I will not go."

In a moment the pumper came and in great excitement exclaimed, "Old Mr. King is dead!" Mr. King was the extra gatekeeper we had employed for the emergency.

When assured that Mr. King was really gone, I suggested that we keep quiet about it lest we get the women on the place excited. But soon the regular gatekeeper came with the same word: "Old Mr. King is dead!"

"Sh-h-h!" I said. "There is nothing we can do about it, so just keep quiet, lest we get all the women on the place disturbed!"

He yelled out, "But he is on my quilt!"

There was much more to attend to than getting the dead man off the gatekeeper's quilt, but we got him off. Someone on our place knew how to get in at the back door of a casket shop and buy a casket. We put the dead man in it, though we did not get him buried for several weeks. Fortunately, it was midwinter.

When I finally reached the school after the planes had gone, I found the girls all on their knees calling upon the Lord. No one was hurt.

While I stood in that basement, the second bomb was dropped in the yard just where I would have been, had I been a hardheaded old maid who did not take suggestions! That bomb had fallen about ten feet from our kindergarten building, which had a huge U. S. flag lying flat on the roof. The well tower had a flying flag; so did the church, twenty yards away. Since Japan at that time was trying to get the United States to approve of her so-called holy war upon China (her declared purpose being to exterminate communism), we knew that the bombs that fell upon our property were accidental.

I was cut off from our mission secretary in Shanghai, but I got a telegram to the west to the American Consul in Hankow to report the bombing. I also sent a note by messenger to the Presbyterian mission in the south suburb of our city. It did not take Dean Walter and Mr. D'Olive long to walk that two miles. They soon returned home to see if they could make a place for the dozen Chinese who were left. There was no question about me.

The women guests had packed their camping outfits and

gone home. All on the place got busy moving house furnishings and school furniture, nailing straw mats over open windows, preparing to leave for an indefinite time.

As we went around busily, the Chinese co-workers would ask, "Why did God, in whom we were trusting, permit those bombs to drop here on our mission grounds?"

I had known the Lord since before they were born and could answer, "We never ask 'Why' about anything that God permits. He knew that we were here and he knew that we were trusting him. We may not understand in this life, but this is not evil. The Lord permitted this for some purpose. He, the mighty God, does not have to explain himself to human beings —at least not now."

In addition to getting the place in order, I had to pack away my personal things and select some to take. I did not know whether I would go west and keep ahead of the Japanese army, or land in a port city or even in America. Therefore, I had to take warm clothes and bedding and a few of my American clothes, as well as all important papers and mission account books.

Though firing a short distance away had been going on all the day before and throughout the night, we did not hear a cannon from eight till nine o'clock as we walked the two miles to the Presbyterian mission. But just as we got there, the firing began. Louder and louder it grew, until by two o'clock it was just terrific, but we were two miles away and getting only the noise. With the sudden hush at 5:00 P.M., we knew that we had passed into the hands of the Japanese.

My Chinese friends were given room for their pallets to be spread at night on the cement floor of the Presbyterian clinic waiting room, and I stayed with a missionary.

The next morning after the fall of the city, Mr. Walter and Mr. D'Olive went with me into the city to notify Dr. Rankin, our secretary in Shanghai, that I was safe. But we found that all wires had been cut by the military, who would install their own private lines.

While I was trying to find out from the Japanese soldiers in charge (whose language I did not understand) why I could not send the message, two Japanese military officials came along with one whom they thought was an interpreter. I asked them to go with me and see the damage their bombs had done two days before.

Upon reaching our gate, the three men whom I had left in charge of the mission property met me, trembling. "But for the grace of God," they said, "we would not be here!" They had spent the day before in the basement of the well tower, into which huge holes had been knocked on two sides. As I went on inside the grounds and saw the damage, my heart was singing praises to the Lord that the rest of us had not been there!

Two shells had entered my room. Kitchen, dining room, and bathroom were damaged, and the two bedrooms which had not suffered from the bombing had been ruined by the shelling.

My iron bed was apart on the floor. Round bullets the size of one's thumb were scattered all over the floors, with the partition walls full of bullet holes. We counted the parts of twenty shells which had exploded in our mission property, and others lay unexploded.

When the Japanese officers and I had gone over the place and reached the backyard of the Connely house, looking up at the wrecked roof, one of them said something to the would-be interpreter. He, taking out his little Japanese-English dictionary, turned and turned from one place to another until he found his words, which were: "I . . . ad-mit . . . it . . . is . . . a . . . des-per-ate . . . sit-u-a-tion!" While I quite agreed with him that it was a desperate situation, I was thrilling over the fact that the mighty God hears our prayers. He had guided the hands of those pilots and allowed those bombs to be dropped into our mission grounds in order to scatter us all out from there, that perhaps he might save the lives of some and protect the nerves of all.

7

Life
Under
the
Conqueror

The Japanese came into our city like wild beasts. The soldiers had been granted three days' liberty as a reward for taking the city, but they came nearer having three months' leave.

The Christians asked me to return to our mission compound. Forty rooms in the block opposite the mission were made available for the church women and girls. All outside gates were closed, with passages opened through walls from one courtyard to another. The only entrance to the homes in the block was the front gate by my room, where hung my American flag.

Sufficient Grace

This was the Lord's doing, and it is marvellous in our eyes. Mark 12:11

It was Thursday when I went back into the city to live. The next day Bible classes for all in the block were begun. On Saturday I had paper pasted over broken windows in the assembly room of the church basement, and on Sunday we met there for worship. I used the message which I had been preparing when the bombs struck on the previous Monday. Such a testimony meeting we had following the message! What praise to the Lord for his protecting care! Half of the congregation had to wait until a later date to express their gratitude for deliverance.

During the following days I was busy going out in a U.S.-flag-bedecked ricksha, escorting young women and girls to my place. Some of them had been hiding in trunks and clothes chests and others behind false partitions in rooms. I met those women who had gone with me to the Presbyterian mission, and walked with them through the city gates past the Japanese guards, back to our mission.

Former students who had fled to the country and found the villages unsafe, would notify me that they were outside the city walls but did not dare enter the gates. All that was necessary was for the American to pass with them through the gates by the Japanese guards.

It was interesting to try to recognize neighbor girls dressed and made up like old wrinkled women. One of them cut her beautiful long braids of hair, dressed like a boy, and pulled her mother through the gates in a ricksha.

When our forty rooms were filled, additional space was given on two sides of the mission buildings. I patched up enough of the Connely residence to move back there. However, I kept my room across the street, in the hope that the Japanese would never know where I was sleeping on any particular night. A Bible school was opened for the 150 girls and young women, and other classes were kept going for older women.

During previous wars, I had boasted that I would always go to a port when the United States Consul so advised, lest I get cut off and some other woman be left in anxiety while her husband came to rescue me. Two weeks after the bombing, a touring car and two truck-loads of Japanese soldiers arrived at our gate. Imagine my joy when Dr. John Abernathy, of the Baptist mission in Tsinan, stepped out of the car! I was too thrilled to be disturbed over the anxious wife left behind.

As soon as Dr. Abernathy heard over the radio from Hankow that our property was bombed, he went to the head Japanese official of the province and requested a travel permit to go to Tsining. The reply was, "Certainly not! Tsining is on the front firing lines!" Dr. Abernathy told him that mission buildings had been bombed and one Baptist missionary—a woman—was there alone and he must go see about her. The official, greatly surprised, said, "I will go and take you. I must investigate the bombing of American property."

An estimate was made for the property repairs and the money handed over by the official.

Mrs. Abernathy had sent an invitation by her husband for me to return to their home with him. But I could not leave the responsibility and opportunity in Tsining.

The Lord gave me the good judgment not to accept money for board from the girls, since the city was liable to get shut up, causing a food shortage. Each family provided for its own girls. Only a man or elderly woman dared go out on the street to bring the cooked food—three meals in one—at noon each day. The courtyard gathering of those with the food, students, teachers, the preacher, and missionary was like a big reception, with all having opportunity to get acquainted. After the meal the guests were invited into the church to hear a gospel message by Mr. Tai.

We never urged anyone to accept Christ, but continued to give the Word until one knew that he was lost and without hope. The Christian girls and teachers daily prayed for the unsaved and asked the Lord to send the Holy Spirit to reveal the truth, claiming John 16:8, "When he [the Holy Spirit] is come, he will reprove the world of sin."

It was most gratifying to see those who were hearing the gospel message, awake first to interest, then to consciousness of sin, followed by deep sorrow and such misery that they could not endure the burden. We gave no personal help until they confessed to the people against whom they had sinned and made restitution where necessary and possible. If, after that, they had not been delivered in private prayer, we pointed out the promises in the Word and prayed with them. What a joy to see the light come into their faces as they accepted Christ as Saviour!

I saw more people born into the kingdom during that year and a half, than during my previous twenty-two years in China. The newly saved were invited to a class to study the meaning of the New Testament church, in preparation for baptism and church membership.

The Lord's Special Care

For he shall deliver the needy when he crieth. Psalm 72:12

In an adjoining home which had taken in twenty of our students, the six-year-old girl got sick. When home remedies failed, the parents called in a Christian doctor. His experience had been in the army only, and after a few days of failure to diagnose the case, he sent the child to the Presbyterian mission hospital. There she was put into a large ward full of children.

At that time, Dr. Scovel, of the Presbyterian hospital, was sick from a gunshot wound inflicted by a drunk Japanese soldier. When he returned to the hospital, he found the child in the final stages of diphtheria. He used his last injection, but it was too late. The child died. In the meantime, the two-year-old baby sister had taken the dread disease. The oldest sister, one of our pupils, had carried the sick child around in her arms among the students.

Before knowing the cause of the death of the child, I went to comfort the non-Christian mother. I found her making little red padded garments for the burial robes. She said, "We will get a casket and bury her, for she was a real person." Then she added, "But I do not know how we will get these clothes put on her, for no one would touch a dead body!"

The Chinese phrase for anxiety is "hang up the heart." Imagine one hanging by a hook in the heart. I urged the mother to "lay down or unhook her heart," telling her that I would dress the little girl for burial.

The father brought the corpse in his arms to my side porch. I put the clothes on the little body, while the big sister stood inside, looking through the window.

The strings of the little cap were tied under the chin, and the two elderly carpenters placed the body in the casket. They were preparing to nail it up when one came running with a message from the mother, "Wait! Don't take the casket out yet! The baby is dying, too!" A few minutes later the body of the baby sister was brought, wrapped in a quilt. We tied it on top of the casket and the two men proceeded to the cemetery.

How we called upon the Lord! Not only did we pray for our girls to be spared, but for the children who had been exposed to the dread disease in the hospital. Just then we learned that an epidemic was raging in the city. Even though we had had abundant opportunity for infection and for a widespread epidemic, not a case of diphtheria appeared thereafter on our compound or in the hospital ward where the first child had died.

Another blessing, over and above what anyone could have expected, was in a very different line—not necessary at all, but just one of the Lord's smiles. I had cool water to drink through all that hot summer. Ordinarily, the ice that was cut from the Grand Canal and stored in straw in little mud huts lasted until the end of May. That year, due to a cool summer and fewer customers, I had ice all summer. That blessing not only meant that the boiled drinking water could be cooled, but that a quart freezer of ice cream or sherbet could be enjoyed daily.

The Lord and I and Japanese Soldiers

Ye [are] in Christ Jesus, who of God is made unto us wisdom. 1 Corinthians 1:30

The first night after the Japanese entered the city, a company of soldiers took up quarters just over the yard wall from the Presbyterian mission hospital. Dr. Scovel, the only surgeon, was operating on the wounded all day and until twelve o'clock at night and had to have some rest. I was asked to sleep in the hospital to protect the nurses. A cot was put into his office for me and the announcement made that I should be called if a soldier should come over the wall during the night.

About six o'clock, while Dr. Scovel was at home for supper across the street, a frightened orderly came running breathlessly to tell me that he had seen a Japanese soldier come in at the front entrance! Grabbing my flashlight, I rushed to inquire of the gateman, but no gateman there! The soldier had taken the gateman's lantern, ordered him into his bedroom, and locked him in. The soldier then went to find women.

On the grounds, there were rooms built around a courtyard with a narrow path entrance. The rooms were filled with the women and girls who had been taken in for protection. When I reached the outside of the entrance, there the soldier stood inside the court. He had the lantern at his feet, his gun resting against the wall of a building, and he was taking off his fighting accouterments.

Shining my flashlight into my own face, I called out to him in English, "This is an American hospital! What is your business here?" I repeated the same in Chinese, neither of which he understood. But seeing my white face, he buckled up, took his gun, and came out, passing only two feet from me. I did not back one inch as he passed by, but gave him another scolding, to which he grunted.

I followed him to the gate, barred the doors behind him, unlocked the gateman, and then went back to see who were in the rooms built around the courtyard. The pretty girls and women fell on their faces, exclaiming, "You have saved our lives! You have saved our lives!"

After our group returned to the Baptist compound, soldiers came day by day on the pretense of observing the school, which was meeting in the church. Either our preacher or one of the men teachers would detain them in the yard until all of the girls could move to the church basement. The teacher or preacher would then take the soldiers to the church auditorium and explain how we worship or let them try to play our pump organ, while the girls went from the basement to the dormitory and from there, by a back gate, through my yard into the basement of the Connely residence, where I was living. Often, soldiers came but never saw a girl.

The married women across the street in our forty rooms were as frightened of the Japanese men as were the girls. Sometimes during a class, a messenger would come running to tell me that the "foreigners" had climbed up on top of the houses, and I would have to leave class to go get them down and out. One day a group of seven soldiers, marching in the order in which they went out to police duty, came in at our big gate demanding women. That time I went to headquarters and reported them, so that did not happen again.

One night after soldiers were moved into buildings adjoining our forty rooms, some of the frightened women next to them climbed up on the housetops and jumped down into the court where my flag was. They were taken up with broken bones. That same night three of the Bible school students who lived over there stayed on their knees until morning praying for protection. Alas, for others who had not been in the class and knew no God upon whom to call!

Christian men and their young wives were refugeeing in our boys' school buildings. By the middle of March, as soon as it was safe for even boys to be on the street, we opened our school. We knew that if we did not have a school by the time conditions were quiet enough for a city government to be organized, we would not be permitted to open.

Mr. Wang, the principal of a former government school, was song leader in our church. He and some other men teachers were willing to teach for only their food. One young woman church member agreed to teach the lower grades.

Soldiers entered the school grounds any time day or night, paying no attention to the gatekeeper. Often, when I would be eating or taking an afternoon nap, the call would come, and I would go running half a block and around the corner to the school to get soldiers off the grounds. One day some of them climbed up on a roof by the school and seeing the woman teacher, for an hour and a half demanded, "The woman with the glasses." I was able to get her over to my house in safety, and she did not teach any more.

Some of the soldiers who were quartered in buildings next to the school, often climbed up on our kitchen and jumped down into the schoolyard, frightening teachers, pupils, and refugees. They stood on the kitchen roof so much that we decided to take the kitchen down and build up the wall so high that they could not get over it.

Mud bricks were bought and masons employed, but the Japanese on the other side would not permit them to work. The workers sent for me. I had to climb up on the roof and stand there by the hour to keep the soldiers off the masons while they built up the wall.

Some of the soldiers came and talked in their "unknown tongue" at me, but I pretended I did not see or hear them. Others of higher rank came and ranted even louder, but I paid no attention. I was busy as could be talking Chinese to the workmen—as if I had to tell a Chinese mason how to lay mud bricks! When it began to rain, Mrs. Liu, a refugee living in the schoolyard, brought her warm Chinese garment and big umbrella for me. All day I stood on the roof until the wall was finished and the kitchen taken down.

Two or three weeks after Tsining fell to the Japanese, the Chinese tried to retake it and fought for a month. The firing was so terrific that for ten days the girls could not cross the grounds to the church basement for classes. At night they would come into my house and sit on the floor and sing while I played the piano to keep them from hearing the roar of the cannon.

During those days, Mr. Tai, the preacher, came over to get help from the commentaries on the book of Revelation. For several years we had been studying the Bible book by book in our morning Bible class and had reached the last one. The only time Mr. Tai and I had for this class preparation was during that ten days of siege. As I would silently read, then put into Chinese anything that I thought would be helpful, Mr. Tai would write it down if he liked it.

We were trusting the Lord to take care of us, but I assure

you that we, at the same time, were giving him our utmost co-operation. We wanted a brick-wall partition between us and the guns, which meant frequently moving from one room to another. One day the firing got so bad, coming from all directions, that we had to go to the basement. Too many frightened people, excited children, and crying babies were there for us to concentrate on the wonders of the Revelation. It seemed that we were right in the midst of some of the horrors prophesied.

One night during that ten-day siege, I went to bed in a south room; and when the firing started from the south side of the city, I moved to the north room. (The east room had been too badly damaged by the bombing to be used.) After a while the firing started from the north side and I went back to the south room. Of course, I was not sleeping for the noise. When I had changed rooms five times, I took my bedding downstairs and slept on the sofa. I was so pleased that I did not try the upstairs again for a week. But the roaring cannon, bursting shells, sputtering machine guns, crackling rifles, and whizzing bullets were not conducive to sleep.

However, one night I lay down on that sofa, went sound asleep, and did not awake until morning. I remarked to one in the basement how wonderful it had been to have a quiet night when we could sleep. He replied, "Quiet? It has been the worst night we have had! No one on the place slept a wink!"

After breakfast, when having my quiet time with the Lord, I looked at the Woman's Missionary Union prayer calendar and there saw my name. So while the war raged, people all over our Southland had been talking to the God of the universe about Bertha Smith, and he had listened and given me just what I needed: ability to sleep like a baby.

The Lord not only kept me in mental rest, but also kept my heart in perfect peace all the war days. I came to know what the Holy Spirit, speaking through Paul, meant by "the peace of God, which passeth all understanding!" No *human* mind can understand how one is kept in perfect calm, regardless of all that may be taking place around her. The hymn that I sang daily was:

Peace, perfect peace, in this dark world of sin?
The blood of Jesus whispers peace within.

Peace, perfect peace, by thronging duties pressed?
To do the will of Jesus, this is rest.

Peace, perfect peace, with sorrows surging round?
On Jesus' bosom naught but calm is found.

Peace, perfect peace, with loved ones far away?
In Jesus' keeping we are safe, and they.

Peace, perfect peace, our future all unknown?
Jesus we know, and He is on the throne.

Peace, perfect peace, death shadowing us and ours?
Jesus has vanquished death and all its powers.

Co-workers Return

My servants shall sing for joy of heart. Isaiah 65:14

In March when trains were running again, we invited Dr. Abernathy to come baptize the large number who were awaiting the presence of an ordained minister. What a joy it was to listen to the testimonies of those who had been born of the Spirit and had become grounded in the truths of the New Testament church!

I was fortunate in having Dr. Abernathy's help in planning for property repairs, too. No building materials were on the market, but we trusted the Lord and started getting our buildings back in shape. We found that merchants had buried glass in the ground and had hidden essential hardware. These they brought out secretly as we needed them.

From March until September the mission grounds were filled with masons, carpenters, and painters. There was a stack of good bricks here, broken ones over there, tiles to be used in one pile and those to be discarded in another, with broken doors and windows, good and bad ones separated. Only narrow paths were left between the heaps, by which we could get to the church and school to classes. We were amazed at how the Lord not only provided the materials needed but gave the necessary patience to all.

The big backyard of the Connely place was never so beautiful. The children's tennis court had been planted in grass after they went away to school. There were flowers beyond, filling corners and along the sides. I invited the girls over three days a week to enjoy the yard, and the rest of the time it was my own quiet walking and praying place. Twenty times around meant that I had walked my daily mile. Along with the walk, I sang my favorite hymns from memory and praised the Lord for his marvelous goodness to me, and for what I was daily seeing him do in the hearts of those about me.

Another way in which the Lord showered his grace upon me was in the matter of mail from home. Having two unmarried sisters whose chief responsibility was writing long weekly letters to me, I was able to keep up with friends, family, and events back home. Every week when those two letters came, my next thought after reading them would be, "I will have to wait a whole week before hearing from them again!" If I had to wait eight or ten days, or sometimes for two weeks, even the double number of letters coming did not make up for the long delay.

However, in the autumn when the Japanese had trains cut off, I had to go six weeks without a letter, and every day was as if I had had my home mail the day before. After our city fell to the Japanese, we had no mail for ten weeks, but still the Lord so controlled my heart and mind that I was content without letters. This was the preparation for the time later when I would be interned and receive no mail for ten months.

By September the city again had an organized government. Japanese soldiers were under control to the extent that girls of grade-school age could go safely on the street the half block to our school, and others could come from their homes with escorts. Buildings were repaired, woodwork painted, debris removed, and two full schools opened. The nine months of Bible school had prepared young women, who formerly had been public school teachers, now to take responsibility in our own grade school, with a radiance that comes only from fellowship with the living Lord.

To my surprise and great joy, a letter came announcing the arrival of the Connelys in Tsingtau, after two and a half years in America. However, they expressed doubt as to their being able to secure a travel pass to come interior. Just one week later one of our church members came on his bicycle, too excited to talk, trying to tell me that the Connelys had gotten to the Tsining railway station. By the time he had finished, the Presbyterian mission car rolled up to our gate with them. What rejoicing! They said, "You do not look tired!" And I was not! Had not my Lord said in Deuteronomy 33:25, "As thy days, so shall thy strength be"!

8

Internment
and
Repatriation

After Dr. and Mrs. Connely returned to the field, I was free to take my year's furlough in the United States. Even though knowing that I would be living under a Japanese government, I was eager to get back to work with the Chinese, whose hearts were so open to the gospel message. After four years under the new regime, we had become accustomed to minor restrictions and accepted with gratitude the opportunity of continuing church and school work.

On the morning of December 8, 1941, Japanese soldiers came to the school and asked me to take the Chinese teachers to our residence grounds. When I rushed around the corner to get Dr. Connely to come and see what the soldiers wanted and why, I found him standing in the yard with half a dozen around him, all excitedly trying to speak in Chinese. He said to me, "Go back and get your teachers. These soldiers have come to shut us up!"

Interned

The Lord shall be thy confidence. Proverbs 3:26

The teachers were perturbed over walking away from the pupils to be enclosed in our residence yard. They needed comfort.

I had been in China for twenty-five years and during that time had learned, when anything new and unexpected came up, to get on my knees and turn it over to the Lord just as soon as possible. The problem then became his responsibility and I was saved from the worry of it.

But I did not go all the way to my place of prayer that day.

Just as I reached the door of my bedroom the Lord said something to me. He always speaks to me in words of the Bible; something I know from memory comes to my mind just when I need it. That time it was not even a whole verse, but just a few words that popped into my mind: "There shall not one hair of his head fall to the ground" (1 Sam. 14:45). I said, "Thank you, Lord! That is enough; I'll not take time to pray now. I will go and see if I can comfort the teachers who are perturbed."

It was several days before we learned that Japan and the United States were at war. And not until we were released did we hear of the Pearl Harbor incident.

Fortunately, the summer before, when the Connelys and I went to the port of Tsingtau for our annual mission meeting, we had carried back into the interior all of the money that we could get our hands on. The Connelys had drawn on a family inheritance, and the Lord had performed a little miracle in order for me to have money.

My second summer in China I had bought, with funds from home, a large building lot at the summer resort, Peitaiho, hoping to have a few weeks' rest in a cottage each summer. Soon afterwards financial conditions became so strained in South Carolina that I just waited until times got better to send for money to build the cottage. The better times did not come, and I never built, but kept the lot.

The summer of 1941, when I put the lot on sale, the manager of the resort just made fun of me in his letter for thinking that property in Peitaiho could be sold after the resort had been taken over by the Japanese. However, I am not to be laughed at if I have the Lord on my side. I turned the lot over to him, asking him to raise up someone to buy just at the time when he knew that I would need money most. Within a few weeks a German businessman in Shanghai bought the lot. I received a good price, considering the times, and I went back into Tsining with all of those paper bills inside my blouse.

My first move, upon being interned, was to dismiss the cook. I would have time now for such essentially feminine pursuits as cooking and housecleaning. The Connelys and I decided to eat lunch together each day, which was our main meal. So as not to be a drain on either pantry, I, being one, ate with them two days; and they, being two, came to my house the third day. While we economized, we had the food that we needed. We never dreamed of anything but living there on what money we had for the duration of the war. We expected that to be three or four years. Mary Connely and I vied with each other in trying to make the best casserole dish with half a pound of meat.

I bought one pint of milk a day from a German woman. Out of that, I used milk in my cooking, every other day drank a not-too-full glass of milk for supper, and churned and made butter! But I did not have buttermilk. I saved the cream from the milk, and every few days when I went out for my walk around the tennis court, I took a glass fruit jar with cold boiled water and the few days' accumulation of cream. As I walked, I shook the jar until I had a little butter, which lasted for three suppers if I didn't spread it on too thick. I had a supply of margarine for breakfast and did not need butter at noon when I was having meat!

I was so afraid of wasting time, with nothing definite to do, that I made out a daily schedule. During the forenoon, after finishing my Bible study at eight o'clock, I listed nothing but prayer. I had chosen the Lord's will earlier in regard to either returning to the United States or going to West China in an effort to keep ahead of the Japanese army and continue to work with the Chinese. Not having been led to do either, I had remained in Shantung when the Lord knew that I would be interned. Surely he meant for me to mean just as much or more to the Chinese, confined to my own home and yard, as if I were out in active service.

I had time to bring to the Lord by name all with whom I was accustomed to working, then all other Chinese whom I knew, and all the missionaries. I prayed not only for people of China, but for all whom I knew in other countries. The many acquaintances over in America and all phases of the Lord's work were daily presented to him.

When the Chinese observed the week of prayer for foreign mission work, the congregations would meet for prayer an hour or two each day. On Friday, when they prayed for the whole world, they met all day. A globe was put up and places pointed out as the group prayed. They went home thrilled, saying, "We have prayed around the world today!" Confined to my own room, I was able to pray around the world every day.

The days that it was my turn to cook the noon meal, I had to begin it at ten o'clock, for without American conveniences it took two hours to prepare a meal. Other days I could forget time, and when Mary Connely would call me to lunch, it would seem tragic to have to come down from "the heaven-lies" just to care for physical needs.

In the afternoon I took my nap as usual for thirty minutes, then studied the Chinese language for an hour and a half. With the help of Chinese dictionaries I could, by that time, study without the aid of a teacher. After the study I practiced on the piano for forty-five minutes. This was an especial joy since I had not been able to practice since coming to China. I got out my old college music and had a grand time. When practice was over I went for my daily walk and did the churning! After supper I read until bedtime.

There was not one lonely moment during the entire six months that we three were cut off with each other. We had our own church service on Sunday, sitting in rocking chairs. And twice a week we had a party, which meant that we played Chinese checkers—just three games—and had "light" refreshments.

When we had been interned about three months, the head official, without asking if we had money, brought each of us the equivalent of twenty-five U.S. dollars. He said, "After the war is over we will get this back. You will pay it or your mission or government will. In some way we will be refunded."

The Shadow of a Saint

Except a corn of wheat fall into the ground and die, it abideth alone.
John 12:24

The summer before we were interned, I was greatly blessed by one of the Lord's choice servants of whom I only heard. One of my Presbyterian missionary friends returned from Peking lifted up in soul over the simple messages and spiritual power of Miss Aletta Jacobaz, a young Dutch teacher in Andrew Murray's Bible College in Johannesburg, South Africa. Miss Jacobaz was using her sabbatical year visiting mission fields.

The one message that was reported to me was enough to put me to honest heart-searching. It was based on Philippians 1:10, "That ye may be sincere . . . till the day of Christ."

Translating from the Greek New Testament as she read, Miss Jacobaz said that "sincere" meant judged in the sunlight, absolutely clear, or without wax. It was the custom when too much wood was chipped out of a carving accidentally to fill in the blotch with wax. We Christians are to be sincere before the Lord—crystal clear as he sees us, with no fog at all; nothing covered up, no sham; having nothing in connection with us that is not absolutely genuine.

Miss Jacobaz made no proposition in her meetings such as asking those wanting a holier and richer life to go forward. However, she did give opportunity for personal interviews.

Handing out a sheet of paper and pencil, she might counsel with a missionary as follows:

Miss J.: What is your sin?

Mr. X.: I want co-workers to do their work my way, because my methods are better.

Miss J.: Read aloud Philippians 2:3 and Romans 12:10.

Mr. X.: "Let each esteem other better than themselves." "In honour preferring one another."

Miss J.: What makes you disobey God's commands and set yourself above others?

Mr. X.: It must be pride.

Miss J.: What is the source of all pride?

Mr. X.: It comes from the devil.

Miss J.: Please write on your sin list, "I am like the devil!"

Miss J.: What other sins are in your heart?

Mr. X.: Sometimes when in the presence of women I have lustful thoughts.

Miss J.: Please read Matthew 5:28.

Mr. X.: "Whosoever looketh on a woman to lust after her hath committed adultery with her already in his heart."

Miss J.: Write on your list, "I am an adulterer."

By the time half a dozen sins had been written out and faced, the missionary would be under such conviction that he would soon be alone on his face at the foot of the cross, pleading for cleansing.

What I heard of Miss Jacobaz made me want not only the walk with the Lord which she had, but also the power to enable me and others to see in ourselves all that could not be judged in the sunlight. I am sure that the witness and power of this woman, which was passed on to me, had a share in preparing me for the six months of prayer time during internment, which may have meant more to the Lord's work than any six months of my active service.

One spring day when I was in the yard seeing how many tulip bulbs had come up, Mary Connely came out with startling news. The head Japanese official of the city had sent his secretary to ask us if we would like to return to America. He said, "If you want to go, we will make a way to get you there!"

My instant response was, "Yes, I will go home to my mother! Someone else can count these tulip bulbs!"

It had been a previously unheard-of thing for private citizens of enemy countries to be exchanged during war, and I took it to be a definite work of the Lord upon the hearts of men. I wanted to go home so as to be ready to return when the war was over.

The Connelys told the officials that they would like to stay for the duration of the war, on condition that they be permitted to remain in their home. If there were danger of their being sent to a concentration camp, they would prefer to go home. The secretary replied, "I do not see why you should not be allowed to remain here in your home." The Connelys thought that their presence would be an encouragement to the Chinese Christian leaders. However, the day that I left Shanghai they were put out of their home and sent to a concentration camp.

Three months after the first announcement of repatriation, seven hundred American citizens were quartered in the country club outside of the city of Shanghai. The mosquitoes literally sucked our blood from sundown until sunup. Even after we retired under the nets, they could still help themselves to us as the cots were so narrow that it was impossible not to touch the net when asleep, and there, outside, were the swarms to pounce upon us.

After two weeks of that, on July 15, 1942, the Italian steamer, the *Conte Verde,* of the Lloyd Triestine Line, was ready for us. In order to get the use of city buses to go to the dock we were told to be ready to load at 2:00 A.M. All of us packed up and were ready for breakfast at 1:30—then what a wait, being chewed on by those pests! About five o'clock we got off and went through the silent streets of Shanghai singing, "On Christ the solid Rock I stand! All other ground is sinking sand!"

The *Asama Maru,* a large Japanese steamer, took eight hundred Americans from Korea and Japan, and at Hong Kong took on the Americans who had been interned in Stanley Prison since December 8, 1941.

At Singapore we anchored fifteen miles out while a darling

little flaxen-haired Dutch girl, eight or ten years old, was brought aboard by Japanese soldiers. She lived in Java where her parents had been interned. At the time she was away from her parents in a boarding school. The Japanese were sending her to relatives in Holland by way of the United States.

Imagine our joy upon pulling into the harbor at Portuguese East Africa and seeing the *Gripsholm*, the Swedish exchange ship, awaiting us! It took a few days to get passengers booked and transferred, so we had a chance to see not only the Swiss mission work of the port city Lourenco Marques, but to go out into the bush to visit the work of a Swedish Baptist couple. On Sunday afternoon the local African preacher, in the little mud church building, warmed our hearts as he thanked the Lord in English for our protection and safety thus far. He said to us, "You need not be surprised that the kingdoms of this world are at war. This world does not want our Christ and his gospel. Our Lord plainly told us of these coming events that we might not be taken by surprise."

After Miss Jacobaz went to Korea and after visiting a number of mission stations, about a hundred missionaries were "judged in the sunlight" so that the Holy Spirit could fill them. They wrote to their home churches telling what the Lord had done for them, and pastors became eager to have Miss Jacobaz come to the United States. Following months of prayer and planning, an itinerary of churches was arranged from March until September. The Korean missionaries on the *Asama Maru*, thinking that she was in the United States, had been holding group prayer meetings for her work.

When they reached Lourenco Marques, two teachers from the Johannesburg Bible College met the steamer with the sad news that the ship upon which Miss Jacobaz sailed for New York had been torpedoed. After four days of exposure in a lifeboat off the coast of North Carolina, the charming young servant of the Lord had succumbed.

I had been invited to join the praying group of missionaries from Korea, and when that news came, how sadly disappointed and sorely grieved we were! Miss Jacobaz had known of our many American churches, of our young people, and something of our wealth. She had felt that a spiritual awakening within American churches would result in the lost world hearing of the Saviour. She had been a citizen of the world, carrying in her heart the people of every land, because she had grasped something of the love which the Lord had for her. To her it was not death to die. She would never die, yet she had been living dead for years.

The Gripsholm

He shall give his angels charge over thee. Psalm 91:11

The large white *Gripsholm*, with a big red cross painted on each side, sailed around the Cape of Good Hope and across the Atlantic Ocean to Rio de Janeiro. We had aboard fifty diplomats, including office personnel from South American countries, who had to disembark. As we entered that marvelous harbor we saw in the distance what appeared to be a huge cross, high on a hill above the city. Drawing nearer, we found out that it was not a cross but a crucifix, the famous *Corcovado* statue, 125 feet high, carved out of cold, dead stone. Everywhere we went during our thirty hours in the port city, that lifeless image of Christ was towering above us. To us it was typical of only the dead Christ, known by so many of the people of that great continent.

Our joy was in the reports of those who had come to know the living Lord through the preaching of his Word, and were living to make him known to others.

After a few days of sailing north toward New York, a tiny object was spotted one day on the eastern horizon. Soon hundreds of passengers and crew were standing by the railing, gazing into the distance. In a little while we discovered that our ship had changed its course and was making toward the object. It proved to be the remains of a man-of-war, all that was left, no doubt, after a torpedoing and burning. Our ship sailed all the way around that vessel with numbers of the crew straining every nerve of the eye through telescope, to discern whether or not there was life on the wreck. Only after being convinced that there was neither friend nor foe to be rescued did we resume our voyage north.

One could not but contrast the keeping of the "law of the sea" to save life with the way many of the Lord's people continue on their course, oblivious to those wrecked on the great "sea of life," with no one to rescue!

It was a happy fifteen hundred who looked upon the Statue of Liberty on August 27, 1942. We did not realize then how long it would take the FBI, in screening us, to telephone to all the references given them. We were taken alphabetically for questioning, and I assure you that I was ready to change my name and take any *Aaron* that could be found, before bedtime the third day when they got through with *S!*

Before many words with Board secretary or friends at the Prince George Hotel, I scanned enough of my mail to learn whether or not I was really coming home to my mother. I had left her two and a half years before at the age of eighty and not well and, at the time of parting, never dreamed of seeing her again in this life.

In the Lord's wonderful arrangement, I had four more years at home with her and had the privilege of witnessing the triumph of her faith when her time came to "cross over."

9

Surrounded
by the
Communists

The joy of getting back to China to work under a Chinese
government with religious liberty was unbounded. With high
hopes, missionaries and Chinese church leaders cleaned buildings, opened schools, and started a full program of preaching
the gospel and developing fellow workers. While shadowed by
the fact that Chinese Communists were entrenched in adjoining provinces to the west and north, and realizing that nearby
sections had changed hands from Nationalists to Communists
and back five times, we still hoped that the National army
would eventually be victorious.

Last Days in Tsining

Refrain . . . thine eyes from tears: for thy work shall be rewarded.
Jeremiah 31:16

In the spring of 1948, Fern Harrington and I were in Tsining
alone. We knew that our time there was short, for the Communists west of us, who had been driven back three times, had
returned with a force strong enough to hold what they were
again taking. The city itself was so quiet that our Chinese
friends thought we were safe for a few more weeks. Should
the railway get cut north of us, we could go south, and if cut
on the south, we could reach the coast by going north by Tsinan to Tsingtau.

We heard that Alex Herring had taken his family from Honan Province to Shanghai for safety, so we sent for him to come
and preach for us until we would have to leave. It would be
the last opportunity for a long time, we thought, for a missionary to render such a service to our Tsining church.

Alex accepted our invitation. In about the second church service he overstated a true incident which he was using for an illustration. At the next service, having realized what he had done, he acknowledged it, leaving the illustration partially crippled. This made such an impression upon the congregation that they entered into the meetings with all of their hearts, saying, "This is a true man of God who has come to lead us. He is willing to lose face to straighten out his wrongs in order to keep right with God."

The Lord blessed the results in such a wonderful way that we took it as God's fitting close to our work on that field.

Packing to leave was easy. When I returned to China after the Japanese war, I had left my household supplies stored in Shanghai, fearing that I would not be able to stay in north China very long. I had found a few pieces of furniture in Tsining after the Japanese occupancy of my house, and German people had carefully kept for me my piano and desk typewriter.

Days before time to leave, we sent the piano and typewriter and the few pieces of furniture, which would be difficult to take by train, on a little truck over the border to Hsuchowfu in Kiangsu Province. Our trunks and other furnishings we could take by train by hiring a man who understood shipping and changing trains to accompany the goods.

At Yenchow

I will cause the enemy to entreat thee well in the time of evil. Jeremiah 15:11

Alex, Fern, and I planned to stop along the railway and work as we could, so we took the cook and our camping outfit. Tsining is on the Grand Canal, twenty miles from Yenchow, on the railway running from Nanking to Tientsin. Upon reaching Yenchow we found the railway broken both north and south of the city.

The inns inside of the city walls were filled with military of-

ficials. There was no room for us. We found rooms at a little
inn outside the city by the railway station, and stayed there a
week. The beds were wooden boards, but we had our own
quilts to put over them. I longed for connection with that
Beautyrest mattress in Shanghai, the gift of a friend.

After the first skirmish with the Reds, the Nationalist Army
moved inside the walled city. We went then, as paying guests,
to the Catholic hospital operated by nuns. The hospital was
part of a large plant in the southwest corner of the city, separated from the city wall only by its truck gardens. At the hospital we were given two rooms and meals, the same as the
nuns ate.

The Communist Army stayed in the villages around the city,
where they kept out of sight during the day, only occasionally
firing just to let people know that they were there. Sometimes
a bullet would whiz through our room just where we had been,
but never where we were!

The Catholic mission was in line of enemy guns for two reasons: first, because of its location, and, second, because the Nationalist general had closed the boys' boarding school and
taken up headquarters in the buildings. The general enjoyed
the bishop's home, while army personnel filled the school buildings.

At night all lights had to be kept off, for the city would be
attacked. From the city wall, the Communists' fire was met
with every instrument of war that the Nationalists possessed.
The roaring cannon, bursting shells, cracking rifles, sputtering
machine guns, jarring trench mortars, and exploding hand
grenades sounded so natural that I could not realize that ten
years had passed since I was in the besieged city of Tsining.

For the next six weeks we were in Yenchow, Fern worked on
the Chinese language with her teacher, while I studied my
English and Chinese Bibles, with plenty of time for prayer.
Alex spent his time learning to read and write more of the forty
thousand Chinese characters, and in prayer and sermon preparation.

When the war-thunder began each day at dark, we took our seats on the cement floor below the windowsill. While we were trusting the Lord to take care of us, at the same time we were giving him our best co-operation! Our favorite pastime during those evening hours was singing the grand old hymns which we knew from memory. When we decided to go to bed, we sometimes felt more comfortable trying to sleep *under* our beds, rather than *on* them.

Alex was able to send a message through an army radio station to our mission headquarters in Shanghai when we got cut off in Yenchow. A reply stated that the Lutheran airplane, *St. Paul,* would come for us on June 18. That morning at nine o'clock, we were at the airport. We left our baggage so as many as possible of the Catholic missionaries could go.

We sat at the airport all day long, surely under the hottest sun that ever shone in June! At noon the Catholic friends sent out hard-boiled eggs and sour bread that had not risen. (It never did rise and always soured.) Pig lard was the sandwich filler. How tired, hot, thirsty, and disappointed we were at the close of the day, when every plane speck viewed on the horizon had proved to be a buzzard!

I had left the mission heavyhearted that morning, for day after day I had been teaching the nineteen-year-old broker, who was to accompany our baggage, about his own sin and the loving Saviour. While he had professed to "believe," we had seen no signs of his having passed from death unto life. I knew that when the Communists took the city they would force him into their army, and he might lose his life without being saved!

The comforting thought to me was that we could wait a few more days for the plane if, in that time, the young broker, Ming Kuang (meaning "Bright Light"), could be saved. The next day indeed he did become "Light," for he passed out of darkness into light, and Christ who is the Light of life took his rightful place upon the throne of that heart!

A German Protestant family of five, and their Chinese language teacher and her daughter from another city, were at the

Catholic mission also. They were provided for by the priests in the boys' school buildings. On Sunday mornings we had Sunday school and church service and, on Wednesdays, prayer meeting—all out in the barnyard. The cook, broker, and teacher lived out there, looking after our things and sleeping in the hay. At the close of the next Sunday morning service after Bright Light was saved, he arose and, with a glowing face, praised the Lord for having been received into the kingdom of God.

The head of the Catholic mission was an attractive German priest about thirty-five, who spoke English. He often came over for visits with us, and especially enjoyed talking with Alex. On his visit following Bright Light's testimony, I told him of Ming Kuang's new experience with the Lord, with all the delight that I would have related a conversion to a Baptist preacher. The priest asked one question after another, which Alex answered.

Even though our time in Yenchow stretched out to weeks, and the plane never came for us, our disappointment proved the salvation of one and gave opportunity to witness to others.

We did not go on the streets those days. They were too crowded with soldiers. We could not go in the vegetable gardens because they were surrounded by fences with locked gates to keep soldiers out. So the only place left to which we could walk for exercise and diversion was the barnyard.

Fern found some yarn and knitting needles in her trunk and taught Alex to knit for recreation. He laughed at himself as he began to learn, but he kept at it until he had finished knitting a darling little light blue sweater with white border, for his baby in Shanghai.

He made a chess board on the side of his suitcase, and, out of cheap Chinese laundry soap, carved chessmen. Fern had some paints, so she colored half of the chessmen black. They looked like the real thing. Alex taught Fern to play. I tried once but was too dumb to learn in the time that I was willing to give to it.

Fern and I had an outing once a week when we went to the "beauty parlor." The cook's big cooking pot in the barnyard full of hot water for a shampoo made us beautiful enough. There was no hot water in the hospital. While at the "beauty parlor," we enjoyed seeing the parachutes from the Nationalist planes come down. Sometimes several a day came in, bringing money, rice for the army, and vegetables for the general.

On the Fourth of July, the only American priest in the mission came to have dinner with us as a surprise. He had grown up in a German community in Minnesota, and while he was more German than American, we enjoyed having with us one who knew of our Independence Day. Was he surprised over the kind of food we were eating! He did not know that his telling the head of the hospital that he wanted to lunch with us had meant a better-than-usual meal, with a "special"—a can of Del Monte peaches for dessert.

I have never seen food so ruined in a kitchen! However, we were given the same fare that the sisters lived on. From the abundant gardens the only vegetable that came to us was cabbage which had been boiled for three hours into a reddish pulp. The rice was always sweetened. We would not have eaten those awful starched puddings had we not been so hungry.

I lost fifteen pounds in the six weeks. Alex got sick and asked for rice gruel. It tasted so good that we asked for gruel every day for supper. One day the cook served the starch which had been made for the white bibs and headgear of the sisters. This was an accident, of course. What so grieved us was that this fare was the year-in-and-year-out diet of the sisters. The German family who was eating with the priests across the street reported a variety of good food plus all the vegetables from the garden.

The head priest feared for our safety because we were Americans. Since our government was an ally of Nationalist China, he thought the Communists would make it hard for us if they should take the city. When the city did fall to them, he suggested that Fern and I borrow nuns' costumes and wear them out, so as to be taken for Germans. We just thanked him with a smile. When he had gone, Fern exclaimed, "Now, what if we should dress up as nuns and something happened to us on the way, and we had to go up to greet St. Peter!"

Since the Lord had let us be born in America and enjoy all the privileges of that country, we would accept on the way what ignominy or suffering that might come to us. Anyway, since we were trusting the Lord to take care of us, we thought that he could look out for an American just as easily as for a German.

Alex had come to Tsining when the weather was still cool; so had brought only winter clothes. By July the weather was H-O-T! The sewing machine of the girls' school had been put in the hospital hall just outside of Fern's and my room, as a safer place to keep it. Having a piece of khaki in her trunk, Fern used the machine to make Alex two pairs of shorts. Then she found other material and made a pretty dress for herself.

Alex was so comfortable and pleased with his shorts that Fern wanted to make another pair for him. After her morning study she went over to the barn to her trunk to look for material that could be used. She had just gotten her trunk open and the trays out when the Communists let loose everything they had against our corner of the city.

Fern and the cook rushed into a haystack in the big barn and stayed there until after sundown. Alex and I were over at the hospital praying for a lull so that Fern could get back; and, needless to say, she and the cook, the teacher, and the broker were praying for the same.

There was a big recreation field between the hospital and the school building, and the barnyard was beyond that. The shelling continued unabated across the recreation ground.

Seeing that it was getting dark, Fern decided she could not wait longer to go back to the hospital. She said, "Lord, I cannot let Alex Herring, who has a wife and four children to live for, run any risk in coming over here to see about me. I've just got to go back! You know where I am going to be!"

She started out at a rapid pace through the barnyard and by the school dormitories. When she reached the open space of the recreation ground, there was suddenly a cessation of firing. She walked stately, in a ladylike, confident manner, across the grounds, out the gate, and down the street a little way and into the hospital entrance. The heavy firing immediately started up again. Alex was just starting to go out for her.

The continued firing was so terrific that Fern and I moved our beds into a little room across the hall in the opposite direction from the guns. I do not know why we were so optimistic as to think that we would need beds! In a few minutes we had them pushed across double windows that had a brick pillar between them. We then put the table and chairs on top of the beds and we sat on the floor.

Seeing that there would be no sleeping, and Alex's room being exposed, we suggested that he come and sit in our room. He sat on the floor and leaned against a white plastered wall at the foot of the beds. Fern sat at the head of the beds and leaned against that wall, and I sat about the middle and leaned against the outside bed.

All night long we sat listening to the bombardment of the city. The next morning about six o'clock, one of the hospital orderlies rushed into our open door and whispered, "They are here! They are here!" We knew he meant the Communists.

I had known the Lord since before either of my companions was born. I wanted to reassure them that the Lord was still on his throne and was with us, even though all seemed wrong with the world, and we were in the hands of the Communists. I started softly singing that grand old hymn, "How Firm a Foundation." Seven verses of it had seen me through three or four wars before. I finished the first six verses, reminding ourselves that no other promises than those which we had were needed, and no matter what our condition, the water could not drown us and the fire could not burn us; and even when human strength was gone, we would have no cause for worry, for the Lord himself would do for us all that we could need.

At that moment one of the Communists came to the end of the hall and threw a hand grenade that exploded on the cement floor just before our open door, about three feet from me. I sang the last verse under the bed!

> The soul that on Jesus hath leaned for repose
> I will not, I will not desert to his foes;
> That soul, though all hell should endeavor to shake,
> I'll never, no, never, no, never forsake!

It seemed that all hell *was* endeavoring to shake and succeeding fairly well, but our God was there, keeping our hearts in peace.

The hospital staff started for the basement, and all the patients who could, got up, took their bedding rolls, and went down. The nun in charge came by and asked if we wanted to go down, but, knowing that it would be crowded and not wanting to get in their way any more than necessary, we stayed on where we were.

The Nationalist Army tried to escape by the city's east gate and down the highway. They were mowed down by the enemy soldiers who were hiding behind the city wall awaiting them.

The local militia were just not going to give up their city. They came into the hospital yard and started throwing hand grenades at the Communists who were across the street in the boys' school recreation grounds. This bombardment went on for hours, back and forth, POP! POP! POP!

After a while one of those grenades hit the brick pillar between the two windows in our room. The column was shattered, and bits of brick and cement flew over the room. Ceiling and walls were speckled except for one place. When Alex moved, an outline of his head and shoulders showed where he had been leaning. Not one of us had been touched! Miracle!

I can tell you one bigger than that! We then went down to the basement. The narrow hall was filled with patients sitting on the floor on their bedding rolls. All doors on the hall were closed. Along one side was a long backless bench filled with

Chinese nurses who, led by a nun, were chanting their prayers to Mary in Chinese. Alex went into an inner room with Chinese doctors. Fern and I got standing room in the hall, I, next to a full-length glass door and she, next to me, and there we stood.

Not having slept the night before or eaten any breakfast, after a few hours I thought that I was tired. There was a camp chair just opposite the glass door which no one dared to use. I suggested to Fern I supposed it would be all right for me to rest awhile. I had no more than sat down when that full-length door shattered all over me! Had my face been scarred, I would have lost no beauty, but had my spectacles been broken, I would have been ruined. Having been born too farsighted, I had terrific headaches without my spectacles. There was not a scratch on my glasses. Miracle! The Lord was between me and that glass.

After that, I decided that I had plenty of strength to stand, whether or not I had eaten or slept. Sometime about midafternoon, when the local militia had run out of hand grenades, or too many men had been killed for the others to hold on, the Communists ran into the hospital grounds and took control.

A small mine was planted at the base of the double doors of the hospital basement. When the explosion destroyed the doors, one man's head was blown off, and people's blood spattered the walls. Three Communist soldiers rushed in, shooting as they came in that crowded hallway. One German nun was shot in the arm and a Chinese nurse hit in the hand. Of course it was bedlam. Women screamed, and Chinese patients jumped up from their bedding rolls on the floor, yelling out their fright. Fern and I were as calm as it was possible for two human beings to be! Miracle! The greatest of all!

The Chinese doctors rushed out from an inner room, caught hold of the three men, and held their arms and gun. They assured the men that there were no Nationalist soldiers there and that we were all law-abiding private civilians.

The smoke and powder fumes that filled the narrow hall were stifling. Fern and I worked our way through the standing crowd to the other end of the hall where the door opening into an inner courtyard was cracked a bit. There we got some fresh air and a seat on some vacated bedding rolls.

The three soldiers began to question us.

"Of what country are you citizens?" one asked.

"We are Americans," I replied in his own language.

"What are you doing here?" was his next question.

"We are missionaries," I said.

"Don't be afraid!" he said. "We are here to protect you!"

I thought "Sirs, you are going about it in a pretty way!"

Within a few minutes the Communists had moved in and taken over the hospital. The first time that I went out of my room that night and saw the place full of them, for a second I was so possessed with fear that I ran into my room. How ashamed I was of so dishonoring my Lord who had been my protector and my peace for thirty-one years through every ill-wind that had blown!

The majority of that incoming army seemed to be ignorant mountain boys under twenty. They would rush into our room unannounced and peer into our faces, asking, "How old are you?" Asking one's age is a common question in China. One of them asked me whether America were nearer to Shanghai or to Canton!

During the next few days all the Communist soldiers were busy robbing the city of everything that they could use. They knew they must work fast, for the Nationalist planes might come and bomb them out. But while they were enriching themselves by robbery, they were declaring their purpose to make an honest nation.

The mission was turned into a wreck. With broken windows and doors, the hospital began to swarm with flies. Garden walls and pigpens were knocked down, and hogs devastated the vegetables. The air was foul with the stench of unburied dead. In fact, all that appeared the same was a lovely blue sky with patches of fleecy clouds. We rejoiced that it was above the reach of sinful man's destructive powers.

10

Release

When the Communists entered the city, the first thought that came to my mind was, "Lazarus is dead!" We, like Lazarus' family and friends, had called upon the Lord earlier to deliver us. Reports of heavy fighting had kept the Lutheran plane, *St. Paul*, from coming for us, though it could have landed any day during the first three weeks. Since we had been left there until we were in enemy hands, the Lord would, we believed, get us out and win more glory for himself than if we had gone earlier.

The Catholic priests and the nuns asked us if we would like to slip out with them at the opening in the city wall, by which the first Communists had entered. Alex, Fern, and I discussed the matter. We decided that since we did not belong to that city, but just got caught passing through, we should wait there until the Communists set up a government. Then we would explain and ask for a travel permit to proceed on our way. All the Catholic group slipped out before daylight the next morning except the headman. He felt that he should stay and look after the mission property.

The third day after the Communists' arrival we heard that the government office had been opened. Alex and the Mennonite man went to call upon the official, while Fern and I spent the time upon our knees. Our expectation was from the Lord (Psalm 62:5). We thought that it would give the Communist official "face" to expect him to act like a decent human being. However, we were evermore calling upon our God to move his heart to grant the request.

The travel permit was granted, with the request that we tell

our Shanghai friends that the Communists were not so bad as
they had been reported. That was Tuesday. The permit would
be prepared by Friday afternoon and the city gates would be
opened for us to go out at six o'clock Saturday morning. We
would be allowed to take only a limited amount of baggage.

Alex and Fern asked how far I could walk. I replied that
thirty years previously I had walked from Peking to China's
Great Wall. I had made fifteen miles in one afternoon and,
after a night's sleep, walked ten the next morning. Now I was
sixty years old and completely out of the habit of walking, for
during the war years while I was in America I was wheeled in
a car everywhere that I went.

They laughed when I told them that I could walk about fifteen miles. We had 150 to go to catch a train. I said, "But I am
not to be laughed at! The Lord will not let me be a burden to
you! If it is necessary for us to walk out of here, the Lord will
give me supernatural strength to keep up. But I cannot imagine myself having to walk out of this city! The Lord has always
taken better care of me than that!"

We began to search for some means of transportation. Every
vehicle had been commandeered to haul loot out of the city.
With our party of six and the German group of seven, we felt
that the least that we could get along on, would be two mule
carts. I began to pray for two.

Because of the narrow streets and the difficulty of turning
corners in the villages, wagons are not used, but, instead, two-
wheeled carts with large wooden wagon wheels with an iron
band around them. The body sits on the axle with no spring
whatever. Four people can sit on the floor of the body of one
cart.

I did not know that, since the Japanese regime, some of the
carts had truck wheels with rubber tires. Everything being new
to Fern, she had noticed the two kinds. Being humble in her
petitions, she thought that one cart for the whole party was all
that we could possibly expect. Her idea was that we would
walk and ride in relays. While she was asking the Lord for one

cart, she was adding, "Lord, please give us one with rubber tires." I, not counting on walking at all, continued to pray, "Two carts, please!"

We came down to Friday afternoon at five o'clock with no wheel-cart, pushcart, ricksha, or wheelbarrow in sight. But I was still believing that he who calls the things that are not as though they were (Rom. 4:17) would provide two mule carts, and dear Fern was still expecting one with rubber tires, for the Lord knew how uncomfortable that three days of bumping would be!

To the amazement of all of us, the head of the mission asked Mr. Herring if he would like to hire the mission carts. We knew that the barn was filled with army mules, for we had heard them. However, we did not know that the mission had mules and carts.

Mr. Herring replied that we would appreciate being able to hire two carts. However, he felt we could not go out in them when those who were entitled to use them had gone out walking. The priest reminded Alex that his people could not have traveled the cart road and gotten by the guards without a permit. They had to follow the field paths from village to village. Also, he said that he would like to get the mules and carts across the border of Shantung Province to their mission in Hsuchowfu for protection. A price was then set for the Lord's two carts.

What decisions for women to make, when only one average suitcase or two small ones could be taken, and a small bedding roll! We knew that we would never see again anything left. I had been through enough wars to take the spoiling of my goods joyfully (Heb. 10:34), and Fern had spent three and a half years in concentration camp. Even though it meant losing most of her household furnishings, clothes, and many precious personal things, she showed that her affections had long ago been set on things above.

Those two carts! When they were pulled out that memorable morning, both of them had rubber tires! Moreover, one of them had springs, never before heard of in a Chinese cart! As we rode out of the city, the Chinese teacher, Mr. Kao, exclaimed, "I knew that our Lord was wonderful, but I never dreamed that he could be *this* wonderful!"

The three big mules, hitched with ropes to each cart, one pulling in front of the other two, started briskly down the road. But soon we were losing time in getting over rivers where bridges had been destroyed, and across trenches which had been dug by the enemy. When no shovel could be borrowed, we filled the ditches with our hands.

The first day we made only twenty miles, reaching a county seat which had been taken by the Communists a month before. Arriving at the west suburb we passed what should have been a cemetery—but what horror! The little dirt that had been scattered over the dead had blown off. The dogs! And the stench! What did those soldier boys who could not read know about sanitation? Anyway, they had been too busy killing more people to take care of those already dead.

Going two miles farther to the east side of the city, we were in another world. Enough land had been bought by the Baptist church members for a church and for the erection of a little school later on. In addition to the mud-brick church building, they had built five small rooms—three for the pastor's family, one for a Bible woman, and one for guests—and enclosed the grounds in a mud wall.

Our whole group was received most cordially, and within a few minutes the pastor disappeared on his bicycle. Pretty soon a man came bringing on his carrying pole a basket of eggs, eggplant, and ten pounds of uncooked noodles. All of us got busy, and in a little while we were all seated in the yard in the moonlight enjoying a good supper and feeling that we were in the suburbs of heaven!

The next night we spread our quilts on straw mats in the yard of a Catholic church. But what a night with the mosquitoes!

Late afternoon the third day we drew near the first city still in the hands of the Nationalists. Guards on the city wall discerned that we were foreigners and reported to their official, who sent out some petty officers to meet us. What relief!

They escorted us to the only train on the road, the one used to bring ammunition from Hsuchow and take back refugees. That two-hour ride! It was not a passenger train; and, being free, the coaches had not been cleaned nor had the train taken rest stops! However, we were out from under the Reds and within a few hours would reach our friends at the Presbyterian mission in Hsuchow.

Arriving at the Hsuchow railway station we purchased tickets to Shanghai for the morning. After a glorious night with Mr. and Mrs. Dean Walter, we were in rickshas going to the station when we were met by a passenger bringing bad news. The track between Hsuchow and Nanking had been broken by Communists the night before, so there would be no trains!

Back to the mission we went. Within a day or two Alex got taken on a Chinese military plane to Shanghai. Our telegrams had not been getting through, but when Alex reached Shanghai and reported our situation, our mission secretary secured *St. Paul* immediately to fly up for Fern and me and for the Catholics who had reached Hsuchow after we arrived.

11

To
Formosa

When Fern and I reached Shanghai, Dr. Cauthen, who was then the secretary for the Orient, asked me if I would go to South China. There was a need for someone to take over the Kanchow field since the Manly Rankins were having to leave for health reasons. He suggested I visit there before deciding.

When I went to my room to pray about it, I knew at once that I was not to go there. I did not have to see the work. The Lord knew all about it, so the mission treasury was saved the expense and I the weariness of the travel.

Baptists believe that in the Lord's work, the Holy Spirit is to be the final guide of the individual though advice from others is appreciated. Dr. Cauthen counted out Kanchow for me when I made my report from the Lord.

Roberta Pearle Johnson and Lila Watson, of our mission in Shanghai, were just back from a visit to Formosa or Taiwan. When Formosa was discovered by fishermen from Amoy, who perhaps got blown farther out to sea than formerly, they called it "Taiwan," meaning platform in the bay. That has always been the Chinese name. When the Portuguese travelers got their first view of the island, they exclaimed, "Formosa Ilha!" which means "beautiful isle."

Pearle and Lila had been so impressed with the opportunities for mission work on the beautiful platform in the sea, that they began immediately urging me to locate there. My special qualification was that I spoke Mandarin, the official language of China which is used over nine-tenths of China. Also, it had been decreed the language of Formosa when the island was returned by Japan to China at the end of World War II.

For three years Chinese from the mainland had been going to Formosa to take the positions formerly held by the Japanese. When the Communists began to take over China, people daily left for Formosa by the thousands.

When I inquired of the Lord where he would have me go, I soon had the assurance that Formosa was to be my new field of service. Yet, the Foreign Mission Board had said, "No new work," and we had no old work on Formosa. I could wait upon the Lord. Would he change the mind of the Board? In the thirty-one years that I had been in China the Holy Spirit had never led me to go contrary to Board policy. If the Lord wanted me on Formosa, he would surely find a way to get me there.

When the executive committee (Chinese) of our All-China Baptist Convention met in Shanghai, they heard of my desire to go to Formosa. They decided to extend the home mission work of the convention to Formosa and "to take me on" as their missionary if the Foreign Mission Board would lend me to them and continue my support. Chinese workers would be sent over later.

On October 19, 1948, when the little plane on which I traveled circled over Taipei, the capital city of Formosa, the Holy Spirit whispered to my heart what he said to Paul when he was in Corinth, "I have much people in this city." I knew that he wanted me to find them and bring them to know him.

The Taipei Guest House, out by the Tam Shui River, was the only inn in the city where I could get a private room. The Japanese-style inns assign as many persons to a room as can get sleeping space on the straw mats covering the floor. The Guest House of the China Travel Agency was only for transients, and limited the time each guest could stay. But when my time expired, the manager, a Christian from the mainland graciously assigned me a little room which ordinarily was used by Chinese who travel with their own bedding. A narrow bed without springs or mattress—only woven cane like the seat of a chair—a small wardrobe, one chair, and a little table beside

the bed filled the room. There was just enough space left near
the foot of the bed for me to get on my knees.

Dilapidated buses went down the main street and across
the river at intervals of about forty-five minutes, but on no
certain schedule. By the time they passed by again on their
return to the city, the narrow benches along the sides of the
buses were packed and all standing room was occupied. Often
I could not get on the first bus that came by, and had to wait
another forty-five minutes and yet have the same scramble.

The only taxis in Taipei were one old station wagon and two
five-passenger touring cars. Even when one of these could be
hired, there was no assurance of arrival at the destination.

Pedicabs came only halfway out to the Guest House, so I
often walked a mile to make connection with one. Since the
wide street was empty, I walked in the middle of it so that I
could sing without disturbing the residents on either side.

At the close of the third day in Taipei I was tired from walking and walking to try to find a place to live or a center for
our work. I was worn out from waiting on buses or standing in
them, and from being tried by ricksha coolies clamoring for
more money when the price agreed upon had already been
paid them. I was feeling keenly the responsibility of securing
property at once, since tens of thousands of wealthy Chinese
were arriving from the mainland, causing real estate prices
to soar. I was not having the proper food. And one of my two
quilts was too thick for cover and the other too thin for mattress and springs!

I needed a new touch with the Lord, so down by the river I
went. There the Japanese, in their love for beauty, had walled
up the banks and made a narrow park between the river and
the road that ran parallel to it. To the left was a modern
artistic concrete bridge, over which walked Formosan women
with Chinese ancestry, wearing Japanese shoes and carrying
their babies on their backs in Japanese style. Across the river
were a half-dozen Oriental junks in which the Japanese had
installed American motors. But now their rusty steering wheels

sat motionless. Down the river rose the smokestack of an industrial plant. Over the way was a lovely hill covered with evergreen shrubs similar to those of Japan, with a foreground of graceful bamboo waving in the breeze.

The "lawn mower" in the park was not only attending to the grass, but was cutting off the buds of lantana and ageratum. What did a big old *square ox* know about the beauty of a hillside! But the next day when he would pull his master's little rubber-tired wagon over the paved streets, he would appreciate the fact that his hoofs were protected with straw sandals, and that his "spare" pair were hanging from the axle.

Being two days by steamer or a thirty-dollar ticket by plane from my nearest American friends, I was tempted for a moment to think myself a stranger in a strange land! But another thought came, "I am my Father's daughter, out on his plantation where I have a right to be!" Just then he threw upon the blue "screen" facing me, the most beautiful rainbow that I have ever seen—such width of stripes and gorgeous colors and tints!

However, something more than the beauty of color fascinated me. My mind went back to Noah and to all the meaning of the rainbow given to him. For more than four thousand years God had kept his promise to Noah not to destroy his descendants with another flood, and I knew that promise would be kept until time is no more.

What promise would the Lord keep to me? "My God shall supply *all your need* according to his riches in glory by Christ Jesus" (Phil. 4:19). I seemed to *need* a good deal—not only a comfortable place to live, where I could have proper food but, more than that, a place to invite people to come and hear the Word of God. And how necessary it would be for me to meet those who would come, as Paul expressed it, "in the fulness of the blessing of the gospel of Christ" (Rom. 15:29).

God in his faithfulness would supply all of these needs, since it would be for his own glory. As I pondered the trustworthiness of God's promises, I noticed two fishermen pulling in their nets. Arising to see their catch, I caught a glimpse of color on the horizon, and turning around I beheld the glory which the Owner of the Plantation had cast over the western sky. Ascending the hill, I stood entranced by the gorgeous sunset and wondered when the "Sun of righteousness" comes, if his "beams" could be more glorious.

The next day, after having followed real estate men around for hours, I heard of a fair going on in the big five-story government building. Taking my bag of tracts, I went to see the exhibits. It was school day and all the students and teachers of the island were there. When I had taken my stand in a prominent place to hand out tracts with the gospel message in the Chinese language, I became exhibit number one!

Many of the students from over the province had never seen an American woman. When they kept coming for tracts, and I said, "*Mei yiu la,*" a young man standing near asked me where I learned to say "no more" in Chinese. Within a few minutes, we had exchanged cards and were chatting like old friends. He was a professor at Taiwan University. When I asked if he were a Christian, he replied, "I have been wanting to become one but did not know how." All that I could do then was to set my prayers upon him.

At the Bureau of Foreign Affairs the headman replied to the same question, "Not yet, but I want to go to your home and talk with you."

A secretary in the Government Land Office, a graduate of the University of Tokyo, laughingly said, "I am a Chinese-Formosan-Japanese." He was wearing old U.S. army clothes and trying to speak English. Wanting him to become a citizen of heaven, I asked why he was not a Christian. His reply was, "I very hope! You come my house, prayer; I very welcome."

Hundreds of thousands of Mandarin-speaking uprooted Chinese had fled to Formosa. They were torn away from their families, cut to the quick over the way their country was being taken by the Communists, and without a God on whom to call. What an opportunity to witness! Educated people of

China had turned from idolatry fifty years before but most of them had nothing to take its place.

The city of Taipei is laid off like a wagon wheel, with bus terminal, railway station, and post office and other government buildings at the hub. Streets run out in every direction.

Day after day I went to the bus terminal, stood at a loading stop, and took out a tract in Chinese and started reading it. The long line of waiting passengers would look amazed, and one would ask, "Do you know what you are reading?" When I answered, "Yes, would you like to know?" he would reach for a tract and then the whole line would follow suit. When that bus loaded, I moved to the next outgoing one. Often I had a chance for enough conversation to secure a card with address, or I repeated, in my mind, the name and address given me, until the person had turned away, and I could record it in my notebook.

The wife of one of the United States vice consuls, Dr. Scott George, learned of my being in Taipei through my reporting at the consulate for registration. The next day she came with her five-year-old daughter, Lois, to take me to ride over the city. I then had an American friend. With tears on her cheeks, Mrs. George begged me to conduct worship service in English. For a whole year she had heard only one sermon. It was by the secretary of the Canadian Presbyterian Mission Board.

When I secured a house I conducted a worship service in English every Sunday afternoon. I ministered to their need and they to mine. In fact as long as Dr. and Mrs. George were there, they took the place of fellow missionaries.

After praying for several days, with fasting, I went to the mayor of the city and asked him to let me have a building for a church. A Formosan who had been educated on the mainland, he was so surprised and pleased that I could speak Mandarin that he was most gracious. He told me that all the business houses which had been vacated by the Japanese had already been assigned to merchants from the coastal cities of the mainland. They had made arrangements for moving their

business to Taiwan before the Communists should reach their
Chinese cities.

However, the mayor told me I would be able to get a *lot* on
which the mission board could build. The decision of our Foreign Mission Board was not to build on the lot or to invest
money in other property in Formosa, as I might be there only
a short time. Instead, they would send money needed for rent.
They did not realize that no buildings were available for rent.
Japanese property had gone to the central government of
China which at that time had headquarters in faraway West
China. Individuals had occupied all of the houses and were
selling to others for "key money" the right to move into them.

A House

Blessed be the Lord my strength, Psalm 144:1

An old Japanese residence was finally secured. It was the
second one beyond the business houses on Chung Shan Road.
While it was against Board policy to pay "key money," I considered it rent in advance for two years. Two more years'
"rent" was used to make the house over. From its dilapidated
condition, it appeared to have been the first one the Japanese
built after arriving there in 1895. The entire house had to be
refloored since it would not support furniture, and I felt that
I must have my own bed, piano, and desk.

The contract for repairs called for completion on December
20, and I promised to give up my room at the Guest House
on that date. When I moved into the house that day, only my
little eight-by-ten bedroom was floored, and I had to step from
one floor beam to another getting to it.

The cook who had been with me in China arrived with
Joseph Chang, one of our teachers of Tsining, Shantung, who
had escaped to Shanghai. Joseph would be my secretary and
general helper. They came by steamer, bringing my household
supplies which had been left in Shanghai.

For the next three months my cooking was done on three

bricks in the backyard. However, I still had better food than I had been living on during my first two months in Formosa.

By employing an extra set of workmen to begin at five each afternoon and work until twelve o'clock at night, I tried to get the house ready for two services on Christmas Day, which was Sunday, and for a party one evening during Christmas week. Invitations were sent out for both services. Had not the Lord still been holding onto my nerves I could have been buried under that proverbial tombstone on which is engraved, "Here lies the fool who tried to rush the East!"

The Formosan contractor knew only one word of Mandarin, which was *Boo* (pu), meaning no or not. He used it in reply to everything that I wanted done. You may be sure that I got tired of being *"Boo-ed"* at by that man!

Since the partitions of the old house were removable paper doors, they could all be taken out easily and room made for about fifty people. That many folding wooden chairs were ready to be delivered from the carpenter's shop. But lo! the windows were not in. Fearing rain, which would mean cold weather, the English Christmas service had to be postponed for a week. I learned while in Formosa that the heat comes from the sun! Any day was warm that had sunshine. Chinese know enough to put on all the clothes they have, if it takes that many to keep warm, and go on to their services.

At the close of the day on December 24, I went to inquire about Mrs. George. She had suffered an attack of appendicitis and called off her Christmas dinner to which I had been invited. Dr. George asked if I could use a Christmas tree, as two had been given to him. The cook and Joseph helped me trim that tree after midnight. I cut strips of red paper while Joseph hung them on. Regardless of the climate in which he then was, the cook thought a Christmas tree needed snow, so found some cotton and pulled it into little dabs to put on. How thrilled he and Joseph were the next morning to find that, because friends had given me a shower of toilet articles when I was last at home, Santa Claus had come.

The cook said that he would save his soap for his baby. He did not realize that the little fellow would be tough enough to use a bar of Octagon soap before he would get in touch with him again.

I had persuaded the contractor to take his force elsewhere to work on Christmas Day. That rainy morning when I sat down by the fire with my Bible, I was too exhausted for the faintest Christmas thrill. The stack of Christmas cards from friends, which I had saved to open that morning to help make a Christmas atmosphere, did their best for me, but in my exhaustion I was saying, "A place to live is just not worth this much expenditure of physical, mental, and heart energy!"

The Lord came to me again, however, and assured me that I was preparing a house that people might be saved, whether they came to it or the missionary lived comfortably enough to keep well and go out after them. That message gave me so much courage that I did not mind eating a Christmas dinner of canned peas heated on the three bricks in the yard.

The Dentist

Bear ye one another's burdens. Galatians 6:2

A few days after Christmas, when Joseph Chang and I started out to lead a gospel meeting in a home across the city, a young Formosan with agony on his face met us at my front door. Since I could speak neither his Formosan language nor Japanese, all that I could do was to smile at him and urge him in English to come again. Mr. Chang, with the few sentences of Formosan which he had learned, tried to get him to understand why we had to go.

In a few days I received a letter from the young man which led me to believe that he had studied English under that Japanese who is reported to have hung up his shingle, "English taught here from A to K." I did finally decipher from the letter that the young man had been a dentist in Taipei, but in 1945 in the U.S. bombing had lost his right arm. With parents to support, and no doubt a wife though he would not speak of her, he had often contemplated suicide. The greeting which he had received at my house led him to ask, "Can Jesus Christ do anything for me?"

A letter went to him immediately, setting a time for him to come. With gospel posters, my English, and Mr. Chang's bit of Formosan, we spent an evening trying to get him to understand that, because Jesus had settled our sin problem on his cross, he could say to every person, "Come unto me, all ye that . . . are heavy laden, and I will give you rest" (Matt. 11:28).

After a few hours the young Formosan was on his knees calling upon the Lord. For the next four months he came two or three evenings each week. After he had taken all that he could of my English, he would listen to Mr. Chang struggle in Formosan language through a chapter in Mark's Gospel. Finally, since he lived ten miles away, the young man had to stop coming for lack of bus fare. Then, the following summer he suddenly appeared one evening at the Bible class with an expression on his face which proved to all of the people who saw him that "if any man be in Christ, he is a new creature" (2 Cor. 5:17).

By the end of March the renovation of the house was completed. A bathroom had been added, and lo! it contained a built-in tub. It was made by one brick being laid upon another, over which was spread cement terrazzo. Two women had then come in and rubbed with pumice stone all day until the tub was smooth and pretty. Now, wasn't that a "built-in" bathtub?

After the kitchen was added and my coal cookstove was put up and I opened up the boxes of foodstuffs which had been showered upon me before leaving home, I just wanted to cook all day! When I sat down on that comfortable chair, I never wanted to get up! And that Beautyrest mattress—I wanted to sleep on it a week! All the trials—even the "Boo-ings"— were forgotten.

The Sofa—an Altar

Unto him that is able to do exceeding abundantly above all that we ask or think. Ephesians 3:20

I put my name in both English and Chinese on the bamboo fence: "Miss Smith Baptist Mission." People began to come. In addition to the Sunday services, we had Bible classes Tuesday and Thursday evenings.

A few weeks after the Bible classes were started, one of the men present asked how to be saved. Learning that he had no Christian background and not wanting to "pick him green" by letting him make a profession of accepting Christ without really repenting and being born of the Spirit, I asked him to come for personal help.

The next morning at nine o'clock he was there. Handing him a Chinese Bible, I had him read passage after passage showing something of the sinfulness of his own heart in contrast to the holiness of God. After an hour or two he asked, "How can I, this terrible sinner, ever get right enough to have fellowship with such a holy God?" He was then prepared to hear what Christ had done for him. When he was ready to surrender his will to the Lord, he knelt by my sofa and started confessing his sins one by one. Before he had half finished his sin account, there was a knock at the door. I tip-toed out into the hall and said to the newcomer, "You just take this chair here. The man inside wants to be saved. When I get through with him, I will see you."

He said, "I want to be saved."

I answered, "Come inside and get on your knees."

After a little while there was another knock and I tip-toed out again and said to another man, "The two men inside want to be saved. Please sit here until I get through with them."

He replied, "I want to be saved."

I answered, "Come inside and get on your knees!" So three men were seeking the Lord, instead of the one who had come by appointment.

That was the way God's work proved to be on the island of

Formosa. There were always three opportunities to the one which I had on the mainland. And I had thought back there that I was doing the greatest work in the world!

People came for help until I need never have left my home to put in a day's work for the Lord. My sofa was literally ruined by the tears of repentance shed on it, but to me it was only beautifully brocaded. Sometimes a new Christian who had not learned how to walk in the Lord, came back and wept as much over his failure to show the Lord to others, as he had when he first saw himself a condemned sinner.

People who had been suddenly uprooted and torn from all that they held dear needed the steadying power of the Lord Jesus. The few Christians among them wanted mothering, comforting, and strengthening, and the thousands who had lost all and had no God were in bitterness indeed.

One morning about nine o'clock I answered a knock at the door. An attractive young woman asked, "What time do you have church service?" I replied, "Come in and we will have it now!"

Handing her a Chinese Bible, I started, as my custom was, to enable her to see herself as God looked at her, and how man had failed God in absolutely every respect. The young woman, Miss Wang, was a teacher from Peking. She had been reared and educated there and, after graduating from Peking Normal, had studied in Japan. Never one time had she heard the name of Jesus until on the way from Peking to Formosa to escape from the Communists. She had spent a night in Nanking near one of our little Baptist chapels. Being upset over leaving home and lonely, she went to the chapel, attracted by the singing. Seeing the word *Baptist* on my fence, she had said, "That is the same word as on the chapel in Nanking. I will go in and hear some more."

Having just arrived in Taipei, she had no work and no permanent place to live. She was sharing a small room with several others. The money which she had brought was being rapidly spent for food.

After having seen that if she received Christ she must die to herself, she was astonished when I said, "It is not the Lord that you want. You just want his blessings—a job so that you can have your own money and a better place to live." After a thoughtful pause she said, "I must have the Lord at any cost!"

Adding her tearstains to the others on my sofa, she truly repented and handed herself over to the Lord, making it possible to receive him into her heart. When she was linked up with the mighty God of the universe, she was filled with joy unspeakable.

As I recorded the date of her second birth, I remarked that it was the date that Columbus had discovered America. She replied, "I have made a bigger discovery than Columbus! He only found a continent. I have discovered the kingdom of heaven!"

She often came back for Bible study and prayer. How refreshing are the sincere prayers of those who know no orthodox prayer language! She talked to the King of kings as freely as she did to me about everything that concerned her or her relatives and friends. She would close her prayer with, "Lord, I am just delighted to talk with you!"

First Baptist Church on the Island of Formosa

I will praise the Lord . . . in the assembly of the upright. Psalm 111:1

After I had four months alone in the work, Pastor Yang Mei Tsai from North China came over, having been appointed a missionary by the China Baptist Convention. After his arrival we soon secured an old Buddhist hall which had been vacated by Japanese Buddhist priests upon their return to Japan. Soldiers were living in the hall. We paid them to move out and let the congregation move in. The hall was ready for our opening meeting Sunday morning April 10, 1949, and the Chinese services were transferred from my house.

We had not seen the sun in twenty-four days. Day after day of clouds, if not rain, during the winter and early spring, meant that everything that could, mildewed; and all that could not mildew rusted. And that which could neither mildew nor rust molded, the leather shoes growing beards. Alas! the dreary days kept on until the human anatomy felt that it would do all three—mildew, rust, and mold!

That Sunday morning when I was in a pedicab going to the new church, suddenly the Lord's sun came out and the clouds rolled away as if he were saying, "I'm for you!" Assuredly he did prove to be for us. The building had been prepared to seat one hundred on backless benches, the only kind that we could afford. About two hundred people came to that first service, and those not seated were grateful for standing room.

After a few months we organized a church. Thirty-six members from Baptist churches on the mainland composed the charter membership. The Sunday after organization seventeen were baptized. How wonderful it was to have a building, with a regular church program and a Chinese pastor! The church grew and now has a membership of about nine hundred, with a building on a main street that seats six hundred. The congregation sponsors three missions, supports their pastor, assistant pastor, and three Bible women, and gives liberally to the work of the Formosan Baptist Convention. The old Buddhist hall is now used for a mission, with the church continuing to pay a small fee or rent to the city government.

Hopes Realized

What things soever ye desire, when ye pray, believe that ye receive them, and ye shall have them. Mark 11:24

Nine months after I chose a lot in Taipei for a church building, I received an inquiry from the mayor asking if we were going to use it. He said that if I did not mean to use the lot other people wanted to buy it. In order to save that wonderful lot, the Foreign Mission Board sent money for the erection of a little chapel which we named "Gospel Hall."

Within two weeks after opening the little building we had two hundred youngsters in Sunday school. Fortunately, when it rained, we had only a houseful, so did not have to hold classes in the yard. Before the building was dry we observed the Chinese New Year season in February with a two-week evangelistic campaign. About forty of the Sunday school boys and girls filled the front seats and joyfully entered into learning choruses and memorizing Scripture passages.

After a week of explaining the Word of God on sin and the Saviour, I asked for any who wanted to be saved to come forward and wait for an after-meeting. The youngsters were asked to file out of the hall and leave their seats for the grownups who were coming forward. Instead, they marched up into the corner by the platform. When I suggested again that they file down the aisle and out, their spokesman said, "We all want to be saved!"

Expecting some to be saved, I had provided straw mats to be put on the cement floor for kneeling. About thirty of the boys and girls ranging in age from ten to fifteen knelt there with a number of adults and whispered their prayers of confession and thanksgiving to the Lord.

A few weeks later at a Sunday meeting five of the boys and girls came forward. One by one, they were led to the Saviour. The following Wednesday one of them, a boy fourteen, was drowned in a nearby river. His parents, who were Buddhist, came by the next Sunday to tell us of the tragedy and to ask us to pray the boy out of purgatory. How thankful to the dear Lord we were that the chapel had been built that the boy might prepare in time to meet his Lord.

With the week's program of various types of services, we were soon reaching people in the area with the news of the Saviour and seeing more and more people turn to him. We had found in the vicinity of the Gospel Hall only one Baptist church member from the mainland of China. We then understood why we had not been permitted to build there earlier. The Lord knew of the thirty-six Baptists living within easy reach of the old Buddhist hall, whom he needed for the foundation of our first church.

Today there stands beside the Gospel Hall a church building that seats four hundred. The church has a membership of about seven hundred. The members have sponsored four missions, two of which have been organized into churches, and one of those now has a mission in a nearby village.

A New Family

They joy before thee according to the joy in harvest. Isaiah 9:3

When I opened meetings in my little house, you may be sure that I invited the young university professor whom I had met at the fair. After about a year, he was saved and took the name Paul. In the summer his fiancée flew over from faraway Szechuan Province in China. Their wedding took place in the city auditorium where I met the bride and the mother of the groom. There were then three for whom I knew to pray.

It was not many months until that beautiful bride was on her knees by the sofa coming to the Saviour. Her new name was Lydia. She and Paul were then happy in the Lord, as well as being happy with each other. She soon felt at home in the new family, even though her own parents and brothers and sisters were so far away.

After a few months Paul came into my study one morning in great distress, asking if I could see Lydia. She was frantic over the news of her parents having been put to death by the Communists just because they were wealthy.

As Lydia came in and fell to a seat on my sofa she sobbed out, "My parents are lost! I will never see them again! They had no chance to be saved! Not one time did they hear of the Lord Jesus!"

How precious the Word of God becomes at such a time of grief! While not being able to offer any hope for the parents, I knew her Lord would enable her to bear the sorrow. We read comforting passages and prayed until she was quietly leaving herself in his hands.

Olive Lawton had arrived by that time, and Lydia invited

the two of us to her home for dinner that evening. Knowing that the family would welcome any whom she might invite at such a time, we accepted. She and a servant spent the whole afternoon preparing a delicious meal of Szechuan food.

The father, with a doctor's degree in science from a university in France, was a teacher at the National University of Formosa. The mother was a teacher in the Normal University. Robin, the second son, was a university student. A younger sister was in high school; and the youngest brother in the grades. All of us sat around the table together.

Paul, not being head of the house, could only bow his head with Lydia and silently thank the Lord for the food. Olive and I did likewise, making ours short. But the others respectfully waited until all heads were up before taking up chopsticks. I praised the Lord for that silent witness of the two. After dinner we all sat in the living room, where Paul took over, requesting me to tell the family about the Saviour. I did my best to present the truth to their minds, while trusting the Holy Spirit to reveal it to their hearts.

A few more months went by, and one afternoon Lydia came with her mother-in-law, who wanted to be saved. Lydia left her with me, and after an hour or two returned to find the woman on her knees, helping to further spoil that sofa. Lydia went tip-toeing into the dining room and round and round the table, clapping her hands without sound and exclaiming in a whisper, "My mother-in-law is going to be saved! My mother-in-law is going to be saved!" And with what joy and praise the two went home!

The new convert entered a class at the church, studying the meaning of New Testament church membership, after which she was baptized. There were then three to join their prayers for the salvation of the others.

The daughter was the next one of the family to be saved by the sofa, then Robin. There were then five to unite in prayer for the two. All were so anxious over the father that they made an appointment to bring him on a Sunday afternoon for an interview. For two hours we talked and read the Word, but he left without humbling himself before the Lord. For an excuse he claimed that Christianity did not agree with science. After a church was built near his home he went occasionally just to please the family, but showed no interest in his own soul.

Ten years after Paul's conversion I visited the parents in another city where both were teachers in a new university. I found the father with an entirely different attitude. The mother had been having meetings for Christian students in the home, where he had repeatedly heard the truth. Her daily life of faithfulness in arising early for her quiet time with the Lord had made him see that Christ was very real to her. This example, with his appreciation for what Christ had done for his children, four of whom were in America for further study, had led him to begin reading the Bible for himself.

In fact, he was so hungry-hearted that he made no objections to my telling him of his sins. I led him to go as far as he could that day in seeing himself lost and undone before the holy God and asked that he write his sins on paper one by one, and constantly pray, "Lord, show me any other sins in my heart." I left, with the promise to return after two days to tell him what to do next.

To my joy upon returning, I found him convinced that such a sinner as he, had absolutely no hope of getting right with God except through the death of Jesus Christ. He knelt in complete surrender, and after having put his sins one by one on Christ, he received the living Lord into his heart. I left him a happy man!

A few weeks later, after having studied a book on the New Testament church, he went to the nearest church, six miles away, and gave his testimony and was received for baptism.

AUTHOR'S NOTE: My method in dealing with individuals was to have them list all known sin and sins by number. When no more could be recalled, to pray, "Lord, you are light. Shine in my heart and show me all that is in my nature which is unlike holy God."

To settle the sin account, of sin-number-one ask, "Is that sin just between God and me?" If it involves no one else the sin can be put over on the Lord with thanks that he took the necessary punishment for it. That sin is then forever finished and can be marked from the list.

What about sin-number-two? That may have been against some one else. If so, after that sin has been put on Christ, confession must be made to the one sinned against before it can be marked out.

When the listed sins have been thus dealt with and marked out, the next step is to put oneself over on the Lord, accepting his death for that sinful nature which produces sin.

The next step that I advised was to choose the Lord's will in advance for the whole of life and for those related to it. Thus Christ could be enthroned in the heart and the Holy Spirit could be appropriated to fill and empower.

The Doctor

And shall not God avenge his own elect, . . . though he bear long with them? Luke 18:7

A year after I reached Formosa a message came from a man in the southern part of the island asking me to come down and spend a week to teach the new converts who were meeting in his home. I could not go, as I had all that I could do in Taipei.

After another year, the same man sent another message for me to come, saying that those converts who wanted help before had followed a lay leader into a group with unscriptural doctrines. He now had another little congregation who needed Bible teaching. By that time I was more involved in responsibilities in the capital city than when the first call came. Again, I could not go. That group, too, followed a similar leader.

I was asked to go to Tainan in the spring of 1952 to open new work. Upon arrival there a third call came from the same man asking me to come teach his third group. But still I was not free to go.

After nine months we were ready to organize a church in Tainan. We were just as busy as could be examining and lis-

tening to the testimonies of those who wished to join, along
with teaching classes and planning a program. On one of those
busy days, a little man with a black beard got off his bicycle
at my door. Seeing me, he exclaimed, "You are Miss Ming of
Laichowfu!"

My Chinese name is "Ming." I got to change my name upon
going to China, even though I did not get a mother-in-law.
Since "Smith" is not a proper name in the Chinese language, I
was given one of their one hundred family names.

When the stranger asked, "Do you know me?" all that I
could reply was, "It seems that I have looked into that face
at some time." What a surprise when he said, "I am Dr. Wang
who worked with Dr. Gaston in the mission hospital in Laichowfu."

So the Brother Wang who had been sending for me during
those years was none other than the former young non-
Christian doctor who had reached Laichowfu just at the time
that I had arrived there as a new missionary! He had at once
become the burden of prayer, not only of the missionaries and
Christian hospital staff, but also of the Chinese church. After
three or four years there, he returned to his home in Pingtu,
still unsaved, and opened a private clinic.

He had heard only that there was a Baptist missionary in
Taipei named Ming. Not being trained in the Bible, he wanted
help in getting his converts established.

During the lunch together that day, Dr. Wang told me how
he had been saved during the revival in Pingtu, North China.
He saw three paralytics healed by the Lord in answer to
prayer. One of them had been his patient, and he knew her
case was incurable. The miracle startled him to the truth that
Jesus Christ is not only alive, but approachable by human
beings who could call upon him and see him do what they had
asked. This fact brought to Dr. Wang a deep sense of his own
sin in the presence of the living, all-knowing God, and led to
genuine repentance and faith in Christ as his own personal
Saviour.

When the Japanese Army entered the city, officers took over the building as their living quarters. Dr. Wang's clinic and residence had been the nicest building in Pingtu. They confiscated all of his medical equipment and supplies, leaving him with nothing.

When the Japanese withdrew after the war, Dr. Wang had no money for supplies to practice medicine again. He came over to Formosa and lived with his son who was an American-trained pilot in the Chinese Air Force. Dr. Wang and his wife then had nothing to do but go from house to house just talking the gospel.

The city in which Dr. Wang lived was only forty-five minutes by bus from Tainan. Having heard that Miss Ming was planning to organize a church in Tainan, he came asking that twenty-five of his group be examined for baptism and be included in the organization. As most of those to be examined were in the air corps, their only free time was Saturday afternoon and evening. We just had to go, even though we did not suppose that many of the group would be ready for baptism. It was something new in the Orient when three women took a bus to go examine a group for baptism, most of whom were men.

To our amazed delight we accepted twenty-four of the twenty-five for baptism. Their testimonies and examinations proved them so clearly saved that we went back to Tainan at bedtime as if floating on air. We were ready for Sunday!

Today there is a church in Dr. Wang's city, pastored by a university graduate who has finished at our Taipei seminary. The church sponsors a mission in a nearby community where many servicemen are encamped.

Good News

As cold waters to a thirsty soul, so is good news from a far country.
Proverbs 25:25

When I met James Taylor, grandson of Hudson Taylor, founder of the China Inland Mission, in Formosa in 1957, he asked, "Does the name Ma Ying Tang ring a bell with you?"

"Yes," I answered. "He was a Honan man who was county superintendent of education in Tsining and was saved there at my house twenty years ago. What do you know about him?"

"Come to see my wife," he said, "and she will thrill you with his story."

I heard the story a few months later when I was in a southern city of Formosa and was invited to the Taylor home for lunch. Mrs. Taylor told me of much that took place before she and Mr. Taylor had to leave interior China.

As the Japanese Army entered Honan Province, the Taylors left for the west and opened a Bible school in Sian, Shensi Province, and organized churches. Brother Ma was ordained a pastor and became a teacher in the Bible school. The Lord himself chose the pupils. They were refugees from eastern provinces as well as from Shensi.

One pupil who was especially bright did not even know her family name. Both parents had died in a cholera epidemic in Kiangsu Province, and she and her brother went to live with her mother's brother, whom she remembered was named Li. He was glad to keep the nephew permanently. But when the girl was twelve years old she was dressed up in a gay garment, with a flower in her hair, and taken on the uncle's back through the rice field to the city, where she was sold as a "white slave." When older, she was put into the prostitution business, at first to wait on others. Everything within her revolted against such a life. Feeling that she could endure it no longer, she secured poison and stole out by the Yangtze River to take it and fall into the water.

As she lifted the poison to her mouth, she was startled by a voice calling, "Go back!" She looked around and, while there was no one there, again the voice said, "Go back!" Though grieved over returning to the brothel, she was afraid to disobey the voice.

Sometime afterwards a rich merchant from Peking went to the brothel and found her crying. She begged him to take her out of that place. Being sorry for her, he bought her and took her up into Honan Province, where he had business. (His wife and children were living in Peking.)

Still the concubine was unhappy. He asked, "How is it that nothing that I do for you makes you happy? I buy pretty clothes and jewelry for you, provide servants and good food, take you to the movies and theater, and still you are not happy. The Christians are happy; I'll send you to their church."

The Sunday that she went to the little church, the uneducated Chinese preacher stated that no concubine could go to heaven. She did not go to church again.

As the Japanese Army drew near that section of Honan, the rich merchant and his concubine went to Sian and even to the same inn where the Taylors were. It was not many weeks until the miserable young woman went to Mrs. Taylor and asked if it were true that a concubine could not be saved.

Mrs. Taylor read and explained the Bible to her until she was ready to get on her knees at the foot of the cross and pour out her heart in confession. She arose, praising the Lord.

The husband sent for the wife to come from Peking and bring the children to Sian, to get out of the way of the Japanese Army. The wife was a well-educated, highly cultured woman, a teacher in the Peking Language School.

Before her arrival the husband, having been so impressed by the change in the concubine, went to Mrs. Taylor wanting to know how to be saved. After an hour or two of Bible reading he, too, was on his knees calling upon the Lord. Mrs. Taylor said that he poured out such a volume of sin in his confession to the Lord, that she felt the need of a bath for cleansing. The Lord met him. He arose with a heart full of praise to God.

The wife, having heard of the concubine, had purchased a revolver, planning to shoot her first, the husband next, then the children one by one, and lastly herself, thus ending the whole family. However, when she entered the home, the concubine was quiet and humble and kept in the background, giving the wife her rightful place. When the wife saw the change in her husband, heard his testimony, and saw a concubine such as she never dreamed could exist, she, too, went to Mrs. Taylor, wanting to know how to be saved. When she got on her knees and humbly confessed all of her sins, with simple faith in Jesus Christ as her Lord, she also arose a new creature in Christ.

The concubine whose name, "Chu-Chun," meant "Bamboo Princess," applied to enter the Bible school. Mrs. Taylor wrote a note to the husband asking him to release her and let her go to school.

He replied that he would place a sum of money to her name in the bank. She could live on the interest and go to school, while the original would be for her old age. He also said that Bamboo Princess was now free to live her own life, and in the future she would be no more to him than any other woman.

The following Sunday Mr. Taylor baptized the three of them in the nearby river and they became faithful members of the local church.

A few years went by, and at the Easter season, Pastor Ma was off for the weekend preaching in another city. Early Easter morning he went out by a river for his quiet time with the Lord. While rejoicing in his risen, living Saviour, he began thinking of those to the west who did not know the Lord. He became burdened not only for the outlying provinces of China and Tibet, but also for the lands all the way to the Holy Land.

Pastor Ma prayed earnestly for the people of these countries. Then he began to feel that the Lord wanted him to lead in forming an evangelistic band which would take the gospel all the way back to Jerusalem.

While Pastor Ma was out by the river, the Bible school faculty and students were having an early morning Easter service in the schoolyard. The Taylors had a map drawn on the ground of all the outlying provinces of West China and of Tibet. The call was given for anyone who was so led to go to either place to stand on the map in the area he felt the Lord was leading him.

One by one students walked out and stood on different map-provinces. Some, however, felt called beyond the provinces of China and Tibet. One wanted to take the gospel to closed Afghanistan. Another believed that the Lord was calling him to take the knowledge of the Saviour to Arabia to the city of Mecca.

After some months of prayer and study of the various countries and traveling conditions, and of enlisting prayer from the surrounding churches, the group of twelve, including Bamboo Princess, started out. They divided into two groups, one going toward the northwest and the other toward the southwest.

Their plan of work was to stop in centers, preach the gospel until some were saved, then teach them and organize them into a church. One worker would stay with the new congregation until leaders were trained, then go on to the next center which was beyond the ability of the new church group to reach, and there do the same. Eventually a line of churches would be established all the way back to the Holy Land.

As the group went west, they found along the way young people who had gone there to keep ahead of the Japanese Army. Many of them were graduates of China's best universities. Some who were from Bible colleges wanted to serve the Lord through the "Back to Jerusalem Band." As members of the band led meetings in city after city, many young people were saved, some of whom volunteered for Christian work.

When Pastor Ma went to the city of Chengtu to enlist the interest of the churches in the new venture, he led meetings where a great number of college students were saved. Many of these also felt called to preach. Their need for Bible training led Pastor Ma to make plans for establishing a seminary on the border of Tibet.

The last news which the Taylors received from the group was through a China Inland missionary on the border of Tibet in 1951. At that time news came that two of the number were in Tibet. They were having severe trials indeed, having to hide in tall grass by the hour as they tried to travel.

Little did Brother Ma realize what the Lord had in mind for

him, when in that all-night prayer meeting at my house he handed himself over to his Saviour for whatever he might want.

Becoming of Age

They shall still bring forth fruit in old age. Psalm 92:14

"Becoming of age!" What pain! I never dreamed that anything in this life could ever hurt like giving up work with the Chinese and returning home. I was still doing about fifteen hours of work a day, and I never became too tired to get up rested the next morning.

Foreign missionaries are automatically retired by our mission board on the first day of the month following the month in which comes the seventieth birthday. My birthday is in November, and that year November 30 came on Sunday, my last day to work as a regular missionary.

I had been asked by the mission to give my last term of service to teaching Old Testament in the seminary and to establishing a new church in the heart of the capital city. Imagine my delight when I went to visit the building which had been secured for the new mission, to find it just half a block from a little lot I had considered for a church site soon after my arrival in Taipei. In six years' time we saw that the question had not been whether the Lord wanted a church in the center of the city or in a residential section where we had gone first. He had planned for one in each location.

With seminary students as co-workers, it was only a short time until we had a strong church. This group asked me to give my last week of work to leading special meetings in their church. A number were present that Sunday evening who wanted personal help after the service. I reached home at midnight, wondering why November could not have had thirty-one days.

I felt that I was just then qualified from experience for missionary work. The forty-one and a half years had been very short, interesting indeed, at times thrilling, and always rewarding. Every trial along the way had been forgotten as soon as the next person was saved.

However, I agreed with the Foreign Mission Board, that its retirement policy was good. Since the mind that we know with grows old, too, some of us would never be willing to retire, were it left to our discretion.

The dear Lord was so wonderful to me that during the last ten days he moved the hearts of seven people for whom I had been praying for some time, (one of them for nine years) to turn to him. They came one by one asking for personal help. What joy in my sorrow to see them at the airport when I left, praising the Lord for the gift of eternal life.

What contrast in my emotions when I flew away from Taipei to those I had when I docked in Shanghai nearly forty-two years before!

Yes! There would be much to GO HOME AND TELL!